Quick-Start Guide

Could this book help you in your mental health journey? Check off the boxes next to the statements that you think describe you.

☐ I seem to feel emotions more easily or intensely than other people.

☐ The smallest things can change my mood or ruin my day.

☐ I feel like I can't control myself when I'm upset about something.

☐ Things in my life often feel overwhelming.

☐ I struggle to motivate myself to get things done.

☐ My relationships have a lot of conflicts or ups and downs.

☐ I struggle with feeling emotionally safe in relationships.

☐ I feel as if I'm living life on autopilot.

☐ My opinions about myself, other people, or my life change a lot.

☐ I'm hopeless about my future.

☐ I engage in impulsive behaviors that harm me or other people.

☐ I don't have as many coping skills as I want.

If you checked off more than three of the above, we believe this book could be helpful for you. Read on to find out more!

Contents

Introduction

We're so happy you're here. Dialectical Behavior Therapy, also known as DBT, can be life changing.

Because you are reading this book, chances are that you may have already heard of DBT. Maybe you heard of it through a therapist or from TikTok. Maybe you read the *New York Times* article about DBT's creator, Dr. Marsha Linehan, and how her own severe emotional difficulties led her to develop DBT to help others who are "living in hell." Or perhaps you have heard DBT mentioned by a famous actress, musician, or athlete, as numerous celebrities have spoken openly in recent years about how helpful and even lifesaving DBT was for them.

While DBT was originally developed to help people struggling with borderline personality disorder (more on that later), it can be a helpful treatment for anxiety, depression, trauma-related difficulties, general life stress, and more. There have been numerous randomized controlled trials (the "gold standard" of health treatment research) showing that DBT works. DBT is a practical, skills-focused approach that can help anyone learn how to better manage the tough emotions, thoughts, and behaviors that occur in today's world.

Beyond the research and the many testimonials you can find online, we know DBT helps because we've seen it ourselves. Combined, we've worked as DBT therapists for almost twenty years. We are both DBT-Linehan-Board-certified clinicians, which means that we have been intensively trained and extensively supervised in DBT, and that our knowledge and use of DBT has been verified by some of the leading experts in the world of DBT. We've used DBT and DBT skills to personally help hundreds of clients. We've seen the change in our *own* lives from using the DBT skills, and we can't wait to share them with you.

Before we dive into learning the DBT skills, we want to provide an overview of what exactly DBT is and what you can expect from this book, in particular. When on a road trip, it's important to have a map to figure out where you are and how best to get where you want to go. Consider this introduction a road map for your DBT journey!

What Exactly Is Dialectical Behavior Therapy (DBT)?

In the 1980s, a psychologist named Marsha Linehan started working with patients who were considered lost causes. Based on her personal experience with severe mental health issues, Dr. Linehan wanted to develop a treatment for people who were in "emotional hell," struggling to cope with their emotions, control impulsive behaviors, and have healthy relationships. Many of her patients had attempted suicide multiple times and had been diagnosed with borderline personality disorder (BPD), a psychiatric diagnosis that was viewed as untreatable.

Dr. Linehan decided to try a newer therapy called cognitive behavioral therapy (CBT), hoping that its head-on problem-solving would be exactly the help her patients needed to change their lives. Her patients hated CBT's emphasis on changing their thoughts and behaviors, though; they felt she was telling them that they were the problem. So, she switched to using validation only, offering her patients space to be fully heard and have their realities fully accepted. Her patients didn't like this focus on acceptance, either—"basic talk therapy" hadn't helped before, and they were desperate for their lives to change.

She discovered that the *integration* of acceptance and change was the answer. Using the tools of CBT and some new coping skills she created, and then balancing them with validation and practices from Zen Buddhism, Dr. Linehan created a therapy that worked! She named it *dialectical* behavior therapy (DBT), based on the concepts of dialectics—one of which is the idea that two seemingly opposite and conflicting things (e.g., acceptance and change) can be true at the same time.

Beyond the balance of acceptance and change, DBT is unique in the way that it emphasizes and teaches skills in four main areas. These four "modules" are:

+ **MINDFULNESS:** These skills teach us how to take control of our attention and focus on the present, without judging it. They help us learn to accept what is happening in just this moment, so we can respond effectively rather than react impulsively or automatically.

+ **EMOTION REGULATION:** These skills help us know what we are actually feeling and understand why, when, and how we can change emotions. They also offer ideas for ways we can increase joy in life and reduce our overall sensitivity to stressful events and difficult emotions.

+ **DISTRESS TOLERANCE:** These skills are coping tools we can use to get through "emotional crises" without behaving in ways that make the situation worse or create bigger problems in the long run. They include some "quick-fix" techniques and methods to survive the hardest parts of life.

+ **INTERPERSONAL EFFECTIVENESS:** These skills are for improving our communication and relationships. They aid us in knowing our needs within relationships, asserting our limits, navigating conflict, and increasing our pleasant experiences with others.

While we believe that DBT skills can be useful for every single person, we designed this book for people who feel overwhelmed by emotions in some way. Research shows that DBT skills are useful for treating BPD, posttraumatic stress disorder (PTSD), eating disorders, substance use problems, attention-deficit/hyperactivity disorder (ADHD), and mood disorders (like depression or bipolar disorder). All of these disorders include trouble managing intense emotions, also known as **emotion dysregulation**. At its core, DBT is a therapy for dealing with emotions.

We are confident that practicing these skills will help you to build a "Life Worth Living." This term is one you'll see throughout the book, because building a Life Worth Living is one of the main goals of DBT. To be clear, this doesn't imply that some lives are not worth living. Rather, a Life Worth Living refers to one that *you* experience as meaningful and joyful, based on your specific values, goals, and pleasures. (Notably, *Building a Life Worth Living* is the title of Dr. Linehan's memoir about her own journey out of darkness to becoming the founder of this lifesaving therapy.)

How to Use This Book

We wrote this book as **bibliotherapy**, a type of structured self-help book in psychology that is intended to help people with mental health difficulties "treat themselves" without a therapist. The book has 12 chapters meant to be read over three months, one chapter per week, with each chapter introducing several DBT skills. At the end of each chapter, there are "homework" exercises for practicing each new skill throughout the week.

We recommend reading each chapter (including the exercises) all at once when possible, because some of the exercises include more in-depth descriptions of the skills. Additionally, some DBT skills are much easier to understand after practicing them. This first read-through will probably take 15–30 minutes. Some exercises may only take one minute, and some will take more than 15 minutes, depending on which activities you choose. While we have provided some space in each chapter for you to write about your homework, we encourage you to also have a designated DBT journal where you'll have space to write about different skills practices and reflect more deeply on your experiences and what you're learning. We include some additional tips in the Frequently Asked Questions section.

The order of the chapters is purposeful. Each new skill builds on and overlaps with the others, so the book is meant to be read and used in the order presented. (One caveat: if you find yourself feeling so emotionally overwhelmed that you're unable to practice the skills in the earlier chapters, you might benefit from flipping ahead to Weeks 7 and 8. These chapters offer some skills for "calming down," grounding, and coping with particularly intense emotions.) The chapters are organized into four sections based on the DBT skills modules: Mindfulness, Emotion Regulation, Distress Tolerance, and Interpersonal Effectiveness. All the skills we cover in this book come from Dr. Linehan's work, and we've done our best to stay true to the DBT skills as she presented them in two of her books: the *DBT Skills Training Manual: Second Edition*, and the *DBT Skills Training Handouts and Worksheets: Second Edition*. By the end of this book, you will not have learned *every* DBT skill, but you will have learned the majority of those commonly taught in the research studies on DBT.

Frequently Asked Questions

Is this DBT? Will a book actually help me? Is three months enough?

This book is not DBT. True DBT includes four components—weekly individual therapy, weekly group skills training, as-needed phone coaching, and weekly consultation team meetings (for the therapist)—and normally lasts 6 to 12 months (or longer). But research shows that shorter spans of DBT can be helpful, and that just learning the DBT skills can improve people's mental health. One 2016 study by Amanda Uliaszek and colleagues found that a 12-week, DBT-skills-only group helped participants improve their coping skills, decrease mental health difficulties, and increase happiness and well-being. While we *highly* recommend that you try to find a full DBT program if you're struggling with BPD, self-harm, other impulsive behaviors, or long-term mental health struggles, we believe this book could be a helpful place to start for anyone.

I'm desperate for this book to help. Is there anything I can do to make it work better?

To get the most out of this book, we recommend a few things. First, read the entire book and do every exercise—you'll never know what's helpful until you try it, sometimes multiple times. Second, schedule this book into your week if you can. It will help you prioritize this work if you plan your reading and homework each week. Third, think about ways to support and reward yourself over the next three months. You could create a mantra for when things get tough, teach a friend the skills you're learning, or schedule self-care activities to reward yourself after doing homework. There are also several online resources for DBT-related community connection (see "Additional Resources" on page 208). Finally, the more you practice the skills, the easier and more effective they'll be for you. You can download copies of this book's worksheets by scanning the QR code on page 208.

Do I really have to go in order?

Although we recommend reading the book as written, we understand that you may be eager to learn a specific skills area first. We tried to make each chapter stand alone, so you could learn the skill regardless of what other skills you know. That said, understanding certain skills really depends on understanding another skill first. So, if you jump to a certain chapter to start, we hope you'll then go back to whatever you skipped.

What should I do when I finish this book?

You can go back through the entire book again! Most people who do in-person DBT attend the skills group for a full 12 months, allowing them to finish two rounds and learn all the skills twice. Otherwise, we've also included a bunch of ideas in the "Additional Resources" section at the end of the book—books, podcasts, websites, and other resources for continued learning.

The Assumptions of DBT

There's one more component of DBT that we want to mention before finishing this introduction: the Assumptions of DBT. We often share them with our own clients when we feel like we've hit a roadblock during therapy, so we want to share a few of them with you:

Everyone is doing the best they can.

Often when people struggle with changing a behavior, they blame themselves. "I'm just not trying hard enough" is something we hear *a lot* from our clients. This idea is a judgmental lesson that we learn from our culture or families when growing up: we'd achieve something if we wanted it badly enough, and if we're failing it's our fault. But that's not true. Sometimes we work *really hard* at something and still struggle. In DBT, we believe that in any given moment we're all doing the best we can. Reminding ourselves of this belief can be important when we're feeling down on ourselves, hopeless, or self-critical.

Everyone needs to do better.

On the flip side, even when we're doing our best, we aren't doing everything we can to overcome problem patterns or change our lives. Maybe we don't know *how* to cope, and we're refusing to google and find a therapist (or new book!) that could teach us. Maybe we avoid trying new things because we're scared of failure. Maybe we give up after only one attempt at a new coping skill. Even when we've done our best, there is *always* something more we could try, learn, or get support in trying/learning. So, when you're feeling stuck or willful, it can be helpful to say to yourself: "I'm doing the best I can, *and* I need to (and I can) do better."

We may not have caused all our problems, but we have to solve them anyway.

While DBT is amazingly helpful for many people, it's only helpful when you put in the work. Therapists can teach you skills, but they can't use them for you. Sometimes, life sucks and feels unfair. It's up to each of us to take control of the only thing we can control—our own behaviors—and learn how to better manage our emotions to start creating the lives that we want.

Patients cannot fail DBT. DBT can fail patients.

If you put your heart and soul into following the practices in this book and you don't notice an improvement, that's our fault. Perhaps DBT skills aren't right for you right now, or perhaps we wrote in an unclear way for you. We would encourage you not to give up, and to try to find a DBT therapist who can help you figure out why this book didn't work for you. Or maybe a different self-help book, type of therapy, or treatment modality would be a better fit for you. Take heart. We believe that improving your mental health *is* possible for you.

EXERCISE: *Commit to Practicing DBT Skills*

Learning DBT skills can be super tough; you'll have to force yourself to try new tools and rely less on the habits you've been using to cope. But the potential rewards are life changing. It can be useful to focus on those rewards when times get tough. Take a few minutes right now to figure out your hopes for the next three months.

INSTRUCTIONS

1. In DBT, we focus on **commitment**. In this first exercise, we want to help you identify your specific goals and commit to working toward them. Consider the following questions: What do you want to be different in your life? How important is it to you that these things change? How can DBT modules like Mindfulness, Emotion Regulation, Distress Tolerance, and Interpersonal Effectiveness help you?

2. **Target behaviors** are the things you do when you're upset that you wish you didn't do or that cause you problems. For example, maybe you use risky behaviors to cope or purposely hurt yourself. Alternatively, perhaps you avoid doing important things due to anxiety, depression, or shame, and there are things you wish you did more. Think about the emotionally reactive behaviors you personally struggle with.

3. Choose three target behaviors that you would like to change (decrease or increase) during the next three months; we've provided examples on the following page. In the second column, write the current frequency of each behavior. You'll use this information to track your progress after you complete the program.

continued

TARGET BEHAVIOR	FREQUENCY OF BEHAVIOR NOW	FREQUENCY OF BEHAVIOR AT END OF BOOK
Decrease binge-eating	*Four times per week*	*Once in the past month (typically when triggered)*
Increase asserting my needs	*Rarely! Less than once per week?*	*Spoke up six times last month; asserting needs is starting to feel more natural*

4. Next, reflect on a time in your life when you made a big change, completed a challenging task, or kept a difficult commitment. What kept you motivated or helped you push forward? What roadblocks did you hit, and how did you cope with them? Note anything that helped you then that could support your DBT skills learning now. (If you don't have a previous experience to pull from, we made some helpful suggestions in the FAQs on page 12.)

----

5. Finally, write a statement to yourself about how you commit to completing this workbook and doing your best to learn and practice DBT skills. You could also comment on why the commitment is important to you. For example, you might write, "I, (your name), commit to practicing all of the skills exercises in this book at least twice, because research shows DBT skills could help me with my BPD and PTSD symptoms," or "I, (your name), commit to following this book as written for the next three months, because I no longer want to feel anxious all of the time, and I believe DBT skills could help me." Use your own language and make a sincere commitment to yourself.

----

6. Excellent! Refer to this as much as necessary to stay motivated over the next three months. When you're ready, we'll see you in Week 1!

MINDFULNESS

Mindfulness skills are considered the "core" of all DBT skills—which is why your DBT journey starts here. In this section, you will learn all about how to take control of your mind rather than letting your mind control you. Before we begin, we want to clarify that while mindfulness can take many forms—for example, meditation or spiritual practices—this book will focus on unique mindfulness skills that can be applied to managing your emotions. So if you were about to skip this chapter because you're not interested in topics you might consider "New Age" or because you've tried mindfulness before and found it unhelpful, keep reading! Many of our clients have had that exact same reaction at first and found that mindfulness in DBT isn't what they expected. As your ability to be mindful increases, you will enhance your other DBT skills as well.

Build Your Mindfulness Muscle

WEEK 1

Let's start with some good news: you already have plenty of experience being mindful, even if you have never learned anything about it before! Any time you savor a bite of food, focus on the sensations as you get a massage, or immerse yourself in an activity, you are being mindful. Mindfulness boils down to just a few basic principles, and this week you're going to learn all about them and have some opportunities to begin working out your mindfulness muscle.

The "What" Skills: Live in the Present Moment

What is happening right now? Not in general—today or this week—but literally right this second. Bring your attention to your five senses: What do you see when you look around? What do you hear? Can you smell anything, or taste something in your mouth? What do you feel with your sense of touch—your feet on the floor, your fingertips holding this book?

What about internally? Do you feel any sensations inside your body, like your heart beating, your stomach rumbling with hunger, or your chest rising and falling as you breathe? Are there any thoughts going through your mind? Are you feeling any emotions?

The first element of being mindful is exactly what you just did: bringing your attention to what is happening in the present moment. There are three different ways we can do this, and in DBT we call these the "What" skills—as in, *what* you are doing when you practice mindfulness:

1. OBSERVE: just notice what is happening, at the sensory or nonverbal level. Bring your attention to what is happening outside yourself, using your five senses, as well as internally (e.g., sensations in your body, thoughts going through your mind, or emotions you are feeling).

2. DESCRIBE: put words to what you observe. Describe the facts and only the facts, rather than adding anything to them such as your opinions, assumptions, or interpretations.

3. PARTICIPATE: throw yourself completely into what you are doing in the present moment. Focus your attention entirely on the activity rather than self-consciousness or distracting thoughts.

The first three exercises at the end of this chapter are dedicated to these skills. We recommend that you skip ahead now so that you can practice each.

What's So Special about the Present?

You might be wondering why we're making such a fuss about focusing on what is happening in the present. Consider this: When you are feeling really miserable, where is your mind? Odds are that in those moments you are either thinking about the past—something that someone said, or something that you did (or didn't do!)—or about the future—worrying what might happen or feeling hopeless that things will ever turn out the way you want.

Usually, the present moment is at least tolerable. For example, there might be something going on in your life now that is causing you a lot of distress—physical pain, a breakup or conflict with a partner, or something stressful happening at school or work. In this very moment, though, you are probably just sitting somewhere, reading this book. It may not be your favorite book ever (give it time! You're only in Week 1!), but at the very least this moment is probably bearable.

In contrast, if you were worrying about when your pain will stop or ruminating about that thing your partner said during your fight, this moment would presumably be harder to tolerate. Even when the present moment is painful, focusing on what's happening right now can help by preventing you from layering on the pain of the past and the pain of the future to the pain of the present.

Additionally, many people miss out on enjoying activities that have the potential to be pleasant because their minds are distracted by other thoughts. For example, we have all had the experience of not enjoying time with a friend or loved one because we are thinking about something on our to-do lists. In that situation, focusing on the present is necessary to truly enjoy an activity. In other words, mindfulness can not only reduce suffering but increase happiness as well.

The "How" Skills: Focus on What Matters

Bringing your awareness to the present moment is a great start, but it's only half the battle. While the "What" skills offer three different ways to be attentive to the present moment, they don't say anything about the nature of the awareness that you need to have. That is what the three "How" skills are for—in other words, when you Observe, Describe, or Participate, *how* are you supposed to do that?

1. ONE-MINDFULLY: bringing all of your attention to just one thing in this moment, refocusing if you become distracted, and not multitasking.

2. NONJUDGMENTALLY: not judging anything about this moment or becoming attached to reality being a certain way. Allow yourself to notice and respond just to the facts as they are, rather than evaluating them as good or bad, right or wrong, fair or unfair.

3. EFFECTIVELY: focusing on what is necessary to achieve your goals in this moment, rather than getting caught up in "the principle of the matter" or reacting to how things *should* be.

Essentially, your mission in mindfulness is to completely immerse yourself in this one moment (One-Mindfully), with willingness to experience whatever is happening right now (Nonjudgmentally), and with a focus on doing what works (Effectively). In contrast, when someone is unmindful, they are typically not fully present, judging what is happening as *wrong* in some way, or focused on what they think reality *should* be rather than what reality actually *is*.

You will have the opportunity to practice and learn more about the Nonjudgmentally and One-Mindfully skills in several of the upcoming exercises. There is no specific exercise on Effectively, as this is part of using any and all skills!

EXERCISE: *Observe with Your Senses*

The Observe skill helps bring your attention to the present moment through the five senses—sight, hearing, touch, smell, and taste. You focus on the sensory experience rather than using words to describe it. When your mind wanders or starts describing what you're observing, bring your attention back to observing. Don't rush—allow yourself to be fully present, observing with curiosity as though you have never encountered this object before.

INSTRUCTIONS

1. Sit in a comfortable position with a small piece of food. Close your eyes and take 3–5 slow breaths, focusing your entire attention on your breath. When you feel ready to begin, open your eyes.

2. Begin with your sense of vision: Look at the food and observe the color, texture, shape, and anything else you can see. Look at it as if you have never seen this food before.

3. Next, bring your attention to your sense of touch. Use your fingers to observe how the food feels. You might find it helpful to close your eyes. Notice the temperature of the food, its weight in your hands, and the texture on your fingertips, as well as anything else that comes to your attention.

4. Listen to any sound the food makes using your sense of hearing. You might need to create the sounds, for example, by squeezing, rubbing, or tapping the food.

5. Bring the food to your nose and observe with your sense of smell. Notice the scent of the food and how strong or weak it smells.

6. Lastly, taste the food. Take just one bite and chew it slowly and deliberately for at least 10 seconds, noticing the taste. Pay attention to whether the taste changes as you continue to chew. Bring your attention to your sense of touch again. How does the food feel in your mouth? What do you notice with your sense of touch and taste as you swallow and after you swallow?

7. Take your time with the food as you continue to eat it, bite by bite. Is the look or smell of the food different now that you have taken bites? Bring your attention fully to your five senses as you continue to eat, slowly and deliberately.

Did you notice anything about the food that you hadn't noticed before or had forgotten? How does this experience compare to when you mindlessly eat something, barely paying attention until you realize that there is nothing left? When you mindfully observe, it allows you to fully experience the world around you and the moment you are in. You can use this type of mindfulness practice just about anytime or anywhere to anchor yourself in the present!

EXERCISE: *Describe What You Observe*

In this exercise, you will practice bringing your awareness to the present moment by describing what you observe, in words. The key is to describe just the facts, and to be as specific as you can. If you notice interpretations, assumptions, or judgments popping up, you can label them, too ("I'm having the interpretation that . . .").

INSTRUCTIONS

1. On your computer, TV, or phone, find a video or show that you have never seen before and mute the volume. Set a timer for three minutes.

2. Close your eyes and take 3–5 slow breaths, focusing your entire attention on your breath. When you feel ready to begin, open your eyes and hit play.

3. Watch the video and describe out loud what you see. Be as specific as you can. For example, rather than just saying, "I see two people walking down the street," you might say, "I see two people walking down the street. The one on the left is taller, has fair skin and curly blond hair, and is wearing jeans, black shoes, and a red shirt. The other person has brown skin, straight dark hair, and is wearing jeans and a green T-shirt. They are walking past a blue car . . ."

4. Notice any interpretations or assumptions that come up, and label them when they do. For example, you might notice that the people are smiling and laughing and assume that one of them is telling a funny story. Separate the facts—"One of the people spoke for about 10 seconds and then they both smiled and laughed"—from your interpretations—"I'm having the thought that one of them told a funny story."

5. Continue describing everything you see, in as much detail as you can, until your timer goes off.

Describing can be a very helpful way to focus your attention on the present—after all, it's hard to think about other things when you are actively describing what you are observing! Additionally, in many situations your thoughts and interpretations can have a big impact on your emotions (we will talk about this point much more in Weeks 4 and 5). Since the Describe skill allows you to recognize where the facts end and your interpretations begin, it can be helpful for managing emotions as well.

EXERCISE: *Participate One-Mindfully*

Being completely present in your life, fully engaged in whatever you're doing, is the ultimate goal of mindfulness. Whereas Observing and Describing can feel like being outside your experience, Participating is being one with the experience. Some call this being in a "flow state." In this exercise, you'll practice Participating by immersing yourself in an activity while letting go of distracting thoughts or self-consciousness.

INSTRUCTIONS

Note: If you have dyslexia, dyscalculia, or another form of neurodivergence that makes writing backward or counting backward difficult, choose another activity for this exercise, one that you find slightly challenging (e.g., standing on one foot with eyes open or closed, playing a computer game, drawing or coloring). Follow the same steps below, noticing any judgments that come up, and bring your attention back to the activity whenever you get distracted.

1. Sit in a comfortable position with a pen/pencil and paper on a desk in front of you. Close your eyes and take 3–5 slow breaths, focusing your entire attention on your breath. When you feel ready to begin, open your eyes.

2. First, write the alphabet backward. Start with "Z" and make your way back through the alphabet, not stopping until you get all the way to "A." It is not a race—take your time, doing your best to come up with the correct letter. If you find your mind wandering, simply bring your attention back to the exercise. Similarly, if you notice any judgments or reactions—for example, criticizing yourself for struggling to identify the next letter, or feeling embarrassed that you can't go faster—acknowledge the judgment, then let go of it and bring your attention back to the exercise.

3. Once you have completed the alphabet, move on to the next part of the exercise. Beginning with the number 200, count backward by 7s. For example, after 200 would come 193, then 186, and so on. Once again, write out each number on the page, focusing your attention on the exercise if any distracting thoughts or feelings arise.

4. When you have completed counting backward by 7s, begin alternating between letters and numbers as you go through the alphabet backward and count down from 200 by 7s again. In other words, after "Z" would come 200, then "Y," then 193, then "X," and so on until you reach the end of the alphabet.

If you found yourself immersed in this challenge, even just temporarily, then congratulations—you just experienced Participating One-Mindfully! The wonderful thing about this skill is that there is no shortage of ways to practice, and you don't need to set aside time for it—you can turn literally anything you already do into an opportunity to practice Participating. Some common examples include singing or dancing, exercising or playing a sport, or even just spending time with a friend or loved one.

EXERCISE: *Identify and Replace Your Judgments*

In this exercise, you will practice two ways of using Nonjudgmentally. The first is increasing your awareness of judgments by noticing (i.e., Observing) and labeling (i.e., Describing) them. The second takes it a step further, replacing your judgments by identifying what they actually mean when you break them down.

INSTRUCTIONS

1. Before you begin, identify a recent event or experience that brings up unwanted emotions for you. Frustration and annoyance are often helpful emotions for this exercise. Choose something that isn't too overwhelming, though, because it can be challenging to learn a new skill when you're very upset.

2. Once you have chosen a memory, sit in a comfortable position with a pen/pencil and paper. Close your eyes and take 3–5 slow breaths, focusing your entire attention on your breath. When you feel ready to begin, open your eyes.

3. Write about the event or situation as though you were telling a close friend about it. Don't censor yourself—at this stage, we are not asking you to practice the Nonjudgmentally skill yet. Describe what happened, and include any feelings, opinions, or judgments that come to mind. For example, you might write "and then my boss yelled at me. He's so arrogant and narcissistic, I really can't stand him. He just likes to feel like he's the one with the power."

4. When you are finished writing, pause for a moment and once again take 3–5 slow breaths. If you find yourself distracted by thoughts or emotions about the event, simply note them and bring your attention back to your breath.

5. Return to your writing and identify your judgments. Read through what you wrote slowly and carefully, and circle any judgment words that you find (e.g., "arrogant and narcissistic" in the previous example). You may also notice places where there isn't specifically a judgment word, but there is a judgment implied "between the lines" (e.g., "He just likes to feel like he's the one with the power.") Circle those too. If you didn't write anything judgmental, consider whether you might have been censoring yourself, or if it would help to choose a different event. If so, go back and complete Step 3 again before moving on.

6. Now you will restate your judgments in nonjudgmental language. Judgments are often shorthand for three things: the facts of the situation, the consequences of those facts, and/or your emotions in response to those facts (not all three components will necessarily be relevant to every judgment). For each judgment that you circled in Step 5, see if you can identify:

   a. What are the facts that you are responding to here? For example, "My boss yelled at me and said I wasn't doing my job."

   b. What are the consequences of those facts? For example, "It makes me want to quit my job, or yell back at him. I don't want to work for a person who treats me like this."

   c. What are your emotions in response to the facts? For example, "I felt embarrassed, hurt, and angry. I really dislike my boss."

7. When you have completed Step 6 for all the judgments you circled, rewrite the event. This time, however, use your new, nonjudgmental words and phrases in place of the original judgments.

continued

Do you notice anything different about how you feel when you read the new, nonjudgmental version of this event compared to how you felt when you wrote the original version? Judgments tend to intensify our emotions. In fact, when we react ineffectively, it is often because we are reacting to our judgments—for example, to the thought that someone *shouldn't* have done something, that they're a *jerk*, or that this is *unfair.* In other words, judgments usually just pour fuel on our emotional fires, which can damage our relationships and interfere with our ability to change things we don't like. Increasing our awareness of judgments and identifying what we mean by them instead—the facts, consequences, and emotions—allows us to experience the moment with curiosity and openness, recognize the actual reality of the situation, and respond in more effective ways to achieve our goals.

Despite how important this skill is, we find that people are often reluctant to use it at first because they think that we are suggesting they turn negative judgments into positive ones. Trust us when we say that we are not selling positive thinking! This skill is about letting go of judgments *entirely*—not just the negative ones, the positive ones too. Additionally, this does not require letting go of emotions, opinions, preferences, or values.

EXERCISE: *Mindfulness Practice over the Upcoming Week*

The exercises in this chapter so far have been intended to illustrate each of the mindfulness skills. We don't develop skills by doing something once, though; it takes consistent practice! In this exercise, you will come up with a plan for how to continue practicing mindfulness over the upcoming week.

INSTRUCTIONS

1. Review the lists on page 34 of additional ways to practice Observing, Describing, and Participating. Select examples from these lists that you would like to try, or come up with your own mindfulness practice ideas that would fit into these categories.

2. In the table on page 35, write down a mindfulness practice you'll do each day over the coming week. Having a specific plan increases the likelihood that you will actually practice!

3. After each day's mindfulness practice, note in the third and fourth columns what your experience was like as you attempted to practice Nonjudgmentalness and One-Mindfulness during that day's practice (e.g., "I was really able to let go of judgments and just participate!" or "I kept getting distracted by thoughts about things I need to do today.").

4. Use the final column to record any other notes to yourself about what the experience was like (e.g., "I was mostly able to remain present," "I noticed a lot of anxiety come up during this one," or "I really enjoyed that one!").

continued

Additional Ways to Practice Observing

+ Observe the sensations in your body as you slowly walk around, stretch, lie down, etc.
+ Observe any sounds you hear at home, in the park, at a store, etc.
+ Observe something you eat or drink slowly with all your senses.
+ Choose one instrument in a song and observe just the sounds of that instrument.
+ Observe what you see as you walk around your neighborhood.
+ Smell all the spices in your kitchen cabinet.

Additional Ways to Practice Describing

+ Look at the face of someone you know and describe it in detail.
+ Look at something you use frequently and describe it in as much detail as you can.
+ Close your eyes and use only your sense of touch to explore something in your home. Describe everything you can feel.
+ Doodle, and then describe it to a friend to see if they can draw exactly what you drew without seeing your original drawing.

Additional Ways to Practice Participating

+ Exercise, focusing entirely on exercising (i.e., not focusing on your phone, TV, or anything else).
+ Take a class to learn a new skill (dance, cooking, sports, art).
+ Play a musical instrument.
+ Doodle, paint, or color in a coloring book.
+ Have dinner with your friend, with both of your phones turned off and out of sight.
+ Sing a song out loud and dance around your room.

While we won't be asking you to complete this exercise every week, we recommend continuing to practice mindfulness on a regular basis going forward. Many people struggle with these skills, especially when they are just starting out in their mindfulness journey. It is hard work to stay present when distractions are trying to steal your attention—not to mention while you're also trying to let go of judgments! Just like any workout routine, though, what seems impossible at first will get easier as you build up those muscles; the key is a commitment to the process, and consistent practice.

DAY	MINDFULNESS PRACTICE	NON-JUDGMENTALNESS	ONE-MINDFULNESS	NOTES/COMMENTS

Meet
Your Wise
Mind

WEEK 2

You've spent the past week practicing DBT's foundational skills of mindfulness, learning how to focus on the present moment fully and nonjudgmentally. This week, we'll ask you to put those skills to use and start applying them directly to making decisions and acting effectively. To live your life grounded in your intuitive wisdom, use our final mindfulness skill: Wise Mind.

Understanding Wise Mind

Wise Mind is an inner wisdom that every person has access to within themselves. Some might call it intuition or one's "highest self." It is often experienced as a calm, eye-of-the-storm, deep *knowing* of what to do, even during really emotional times. In DBT, we primarily think about Wise Mind as a balancing act between the many "states of mind" that get in the way of thinking and acting effectively. When people say, "I was out of my mind when I did that," they're usually *not* talking about Wise Mind.

Two of the most common states of mind are **Emotion Mind** and **Reasonable Mind**. Emotion Mind refers to those times when you're feeling really intensely, and your emotions are completely in control of your behaviors. It might feel "hot," impulsive, or overwhelming. Rather than you driving the car of your life, it's your emotions behind the wheel. Reasonable Mind is on the other extreme, when all you care about are facts, reason, and logic. It might feel "cold," calculated, and goal directed. Emotions and values are back in the trunk of the car, not being considered at all. Wise Mind is the *integration* of Emotion Mind and Reasonable Mind, like the center of a Venn diagram.

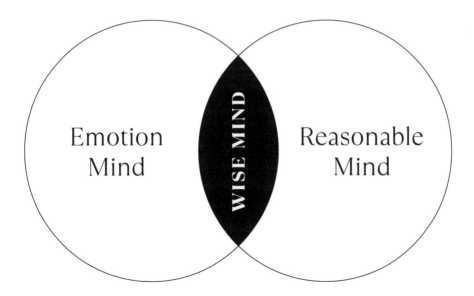

Wise Mind is a bit tricky to describe, because it is going to look different for every person in any situation. One of the most common types of experiences of Wise Mind occurs when you're really distressed and feeling an emotion intensely and still react in a way that effectively balances your short-term and long-term goals.

Let's say you're out with your partner on a date night that you've been really excited about. The night is going well when your partner mentions that they forgot to do something really important that they promised they would do. In that moment, you'll probably feel at least some frustration, maybe even rage, and you might have urges to yell, criticize them, or end the date. But doing those things might be Emotion Mind at work—impulsive, focused primarily on your current anger, and ignoring larger goals (e.g., enjoying the rare alone time with your partner). Wise Mind instead might be briefly expressing your frustration and asking for an apology or recommitment to do the thing, and then throwing yourself back into mindfully enjoying the date.

Wise Mind considers all of the emotions, values, goals, and facts in both Emotion Mind and Reasonable Mind. Wise Mind also might incorporate your intuitive sense of what would be most effective to find a "middle path," sometimes going *beyond* Emotion Mind and Reasonable Mind to forge its own unique direction or action.

The Diverse Experience of Wise Mind

Wise Mind is likely to have components of both Emotion Mind and Reasonable Mind, but it is not always a perfect, equal balance of the two. Sometimes we may not feel very calm or relaxed in Wise Mind. In the previous date example, we might feel quite angry at our partner, and we'll probably have to practice some coping skills before returning to enjoy the date.

We can still feel emotions powerfully when in Wise Mind; the key is *acting* based on Wise Mind, rather than letting your Emotion Mind dictate what you do. In fact, sometimes even *acting on emotions* is wise, such as when we protest because we feel rage about social injustice. In Wise Mind, no matter how it looks, we make decisions clearly, act more easefully, and behave compassionately toward both ourselves and others.

There are several different types of common Wise Mind experiences:

◆ Wise Mind can involve making a hard decision that is the best thing for you. You might have a sense of peace, groundedness, or centeredness, or somehow felt deeply that your choice was "right," even if your decision also caused you or someone else fear or pain.

◆ During a crisis, Wise Mind can allow you to act quickly, intuitively, and effectively, almost without even thinking about it. It can be a gut-level instinct.

◆ Wise Mind can involve acting in a way that gives you joy, perhaps in a way that was a bit "against the grain." Maybe you did something for which you could be judged negatively (e.g., wore a piece of clothing, engaged in a new hobby, came out with a certain identity, or hung out with someone) and loved it or knew it was the "right" thing for you. All these types of situations could be Wise Mind if they helped you build your Life Worth Living (for a reminder of what this term means in DBT, see page 10) even if you suffered some negative consequences.

◆ Wise Mind can also feel almost like "flow," when you feel very focused, content, and calm. It may involve effectively balancing your needs with others' needs, or it may involve balancing your life responsibilities with pleasure or rest.

If you're thinking, "Wise Mind does NOT sound easy," or "I don't have a Wise Mind," don't worry. A lot of people who struggle with emotion dysregulation feel disconnected from their Wise Mind. Some of us may not have been taught how to find it in the face of strong emotions while we were growing up. Our society or our family might have told us we were wrong for having certain emotions or responses, or that we were bad for having certain passions, interests, or identities.

The good news is that, just like we all have a heart, we all have a Wise Mind—even when we're not able to feel it. In the same way that you can use a tool such as a stethoscope to get in touch with your heart, the exercises in this chapter can help you get in touch with your Wise Mind.

Rewiring the Brain

Starting a new habit can be really difficult, and mindfulness is no different. Our brains are biologically wired to prioritize certain neural pathways over others based on our past experiences. When we're in the habit of thinking certain thoughts or behaving certain ways, those neural pathways in the brain are strengthened and become our default ways of thinking and acting. Luckily, these pathways are like hiking trails in a forest; they can be physically changed!

Sometimes when we hike, we come to a fork in the trail. Path #1 is the way we're used to walking—the trail floor is clear and smooth dirt, free of big rocks and branches because we've walked down it so many times. Path #2 is underused—while we can see the trail markers and know there's a way through, it's overgrown with branches and grass. If we're not paying attention as we hike, we'll walk down Path #1. Only when we're hiking with awareness will we try Path #2, and at first we'll have to put a lot of effort into walking it—stomping down bumps on the ground and cutting the branches in our way. Eventually, however, if we keep going down Path #2, soon it will be clear and smooth, and Path #1 will start to overgrow.

Basically, you've heard it before: practice makes perfect. The more you avoid engaging in "bad" or unskillful habits (going down Path #1) and instead engage in a new, skillful behavior (going down Path #2), the more the old habit will weaken and the new behavior will become your default. The more you practice mindfulness, even if for only one minute at a time, the less you'll get overwhelmed by worries or unwanted memories, the more you'll experience the pleasure that life can offer, and the easier it will be for you to find your Wise Mind in daily life.

EXERCISE: *Integrating Emotion Mind and Reasonable Mind*

For this first exercise, we'll give you some guidance on how you might find Wise Mind by exploring Emotion Mind and Reasonable Mind more fully, and then attempting to integrate them.

INSTRUCTIONS

1. Grab a pen/pencil and take a few deep breaths. Choose a current or upcoming decision that would be helpful to make in Wise Mind. Perhaps you need to decide something about a job (current or potential), who to date or spend your time with, or how to handle an ongoing conflict. If you can't think of one, you can choose a decision you recently made and complete the following steps, reflecting back on the situation in order to get the practice.

2. On your paper, briefly write down the facts of the situation. What's going on? What are you trying to decide? What happened, what is about to happen, or what do you want to prevent happening? Focus on facts you can observe, not interpretations or judgments.

3. Next, write about what Emotion Mind says. What are you feeling? What would Emotion Mind look like in this situation? What do your emotions want you to do? What does your body make you feel like doing? What would the pros and cons be if you followed through with any of those behaviors? Could it lead to any regrets?

continued

4. Write about what Reasonable Mind says. What would Reasonable Mind look like in this situation? What is the purely rational or logical thing to do here? What would the most cool-headed person you know do in this situation? What would the pros and cons be if you followed through with those behaviors? Could it lead to any regrets?

5. Now, considering these answers, do you know what Wise Mind says? Do you see any overlap between the two minds? Is there a way they could be combined, such that you get the best of both? Is there an option that balances the pros and cons in the best way for you?

6. If you figure out what Wise Mind wants you to do, do it! If you're still not sure, put the paper down and take five minutes to do something else—go on a walk, watch a music video, drink a glass of water, etc. Then, return to the above questions/answers and see if you know Wise Mind now. Repeat if you need to, take your time, or ask a friend or mentor for help.

7. This Wise Mind exercise is quite structured and analytical, asking you to really think about your various options in the given situation. If you are more of a visual person, you could complete the above steps as a part of a Venn diagram like the one below.

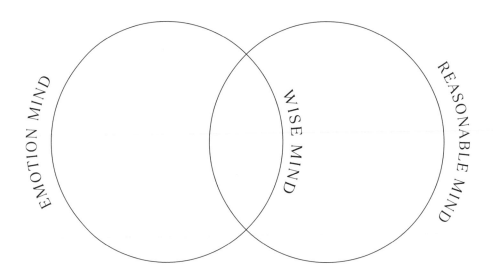

EXERCISE: *What Does Your Wise Mind Feel Like?*

The Wise Mind skill is like riding a bike—hard when you're first learning, but then second nature once you get used to how it feels. This exercise helps you get a better idea of how Wise Mind feels to you by remembering a time when you were in it.

INSTRUCTIONS

1. Sitting in a comfortable position, close your eyes and take a few deep breaths. Using the examples of common Wise Mind experiences on page 39 for guidance, think about any times in your life when you were in Wise Mind. Pick one of these moments that feels clearest in your memory.

2. Nonjudgmentally, write a few sentences about the facts of this experience to help you remember. When and where were you? What happened?

3. Describe what you were experiencing internally during the situation. What emotions did you feel? What thoughts did you have? What physical sensations did you experience?

4. Finally, describe how you know that you were in Wise Mind. Did you notice a sense of peace, confidence, centeredness, or groundedness? What was that like for you? Did you feel your Wise Mind in a particular place in your body (in your belly, your sternum, somewhere else)? Did you know at the time that you were acting wisely and intuitively? If so, how did you know that? If not, what lets you know now that it was Wise Mind?

You could repeat the above exercise with several different Wise Mind experiences to see if there's a pattern for you. Putting in the effort to understand how your Wise Mind has felt in the past will help you recognize and find it more easily in future situations.

EXERCISE: *Breathing into Wise Mind*

One of the simplest ways to connect to Wise Mind is to bring yourself back to mindfulness basics. In this exercise, you'll Observe your breath as a way to tap into your body and access the feeling of groundedness and centeredness that usually accompanies Wise Mind. By connecting to our physical core when trying to figure out what to do, we can connect to our embodied, inner wisdom.

INSTRUCTIONS

1. Sit in a comfortable yet alert position (i.e., a position in which you can stay still without falling asleep), preferably away from people or technology that could disrupt you.

2. Take three long, slow breaths, deep into your belly.

3. Return to breathing normally, and for several breaths, just Observe your breath as it goes in and out. You can even silently say to yourself "in" on every inhale and "out" on every exhale. If your mind wanders into thought, just bring it back to the breath, without judgment.

4. After Observing your breath for a few rounds, bring your attention to a current situation in which you must make a decision or that you want to change.

5. Identify a question related to this situation for which you want to find your Wise Mind. For example, you might ask: "What do I need to do this morning to have a good day?" "Should I break up with this friend?" or "Where should I order takeout from for dinner tonight?"

6. Once you have one situation/question in mind, take three long, slow breaths, deep into your belly.

7. Return to breathing normally. On each inhale, ask yourself your question for Wise Mind. While exhaling, see if the answer comes to you. If in the past you have felt Wise Mind in a specific place in your body, you could bring your attention to this place specifically.

8. Keep asking your question with each inhale, and listening on the exhale, until an answer comes. If no answer comes, accept that your Wise Mind doesn't have an answer yet (or that you can't yet hear it), and try again later.

Breathing into Wise Mind is a useful, simple exercise that you can practice to get into the habit of mindfully checking in to the moment, yourself, and your wisdom. When you're in the middle of having urges that could cause you problems (e.g., urges to call in sick to work when you're stressed, urges to binge-watch another TV episode, or urges to cancel plans with friends), the question may be "Would that be Wise Mind?" Sometimes it will be—we all need to rest, distract, or avoid at times. The goal is to ensure that we notice when these choices aren't coming from Wise Mind, because Emotion Mind has a nasty habit of convincing us to do tons of ineffective things!

A breath-focused exercise may be particularly hard if we're feeling intense emotions. Some people might be really uncomfortable using Breathing into Wise Mind at any time because they find their body or physical sensations too upsetting or distracting. While Breathing into Wise Mind *will* get easier the more you practice it, you can always use something like the "Integrating Emotion Mind and Reasonable Mind" exercise instead.

EXERCISE: *Everyday Wise Mind*

At the end of the day, being in Wise Mind means being mindful. We hope you'll try to integrate Wise Mind practice into your everyday life as much as you can over the next 11 weeks (and beyond!). For this exercise, we encourage you to start implementing some (or all) of the steps to help yourself increase awareness and groundedness in your daily life.

INSTRUCTIONS

For this week, choose one or two of the below tactics, and see how your mindfulness changes! Use the space on page 47 to write your mindfulness plan for the week, specifically noting what you will do to remember to practice and how you intend to practice Wise Mind or other mindfulness skills.

a. Set alarms. It's easy to get swept up in handling life's responsibilities, or to get lost in an internet/social media/technological rabbit hole of distraction. In order to prompt yourself to practice mindfulness throughout the day and week, set alarms for yourself; put mindfulness into your calendar; or set up automatic reminders to yourself via text, email, or other messaging systems.

b. Inspire yourself with quotes. Read some blogs, books, or social media accounts that focus on mindfulness. If anything ever inspires you and resonates with your reasons for wanting to practice mindfulness, write it down and put it somewhere that you will see it regularly.

c. Do a daily activity mindfully. One way to get more mindfulness practice is to start associating an activity you do every day with mindfulness. Brush your teeth mindfully. Take a few deep, mindful breaths before checking your phone after waking up. Take a minute to mindfully pet your cat, hug your partner, or water your plants before you leave for work in the morning.

d. Take breaks. In today's world, there's a lot of emphasis on achievement and *doing, doing, doing.* If you struggle with feeling frazzled and overwhelmed, simply take breaks mindfully, in whatever way works for you. You could practice one of the Wise Mind exercises in this chapter. Or you could simply breathe for a minute. Close your eyes and put your hand over your heart. Say to yourself "just this moment" or "one thing at a time." Stop to smell the roses by Observing and Describing what's happening in any given moment.

e. Get support. If you're really motivated to get the positive effects of mindfulness, we encourage you to find a support system or something that can keep you accountable. Join a meditation group, download a mindfulness app, attend a silent retreat, find a mindfulness buddy, or take a mindfulness class. (We've included some possible options in the "Additional Resources" section on page 207.)

MY MINDFULNESS PLAN FOR THIS WEEK

EMOTION REGULATION

If you feel like your emotions aren't helpful, you're not alone. A lot of cultures and people have come to view emotions as weakness, but we're here to tell you that they can be a superpower. We can only harness that power, however, if we can understand our emotions and actually utilize them.

Research suggests that Emotion Regulation skills are some of the most important DBT skills for helping people improve their mental health. In the next four weeks, we'll be covering several skills that will help you turn your emotions into a strength rather than a burden by teaching you strategies for how to understand, change, and use them.

Understand Your Emotions

Emotions can be confusing. Some people feel super sensitive or out-of-control when emotional, some people feel emotionally numb or dissociated, and others may feel a little bit of everything in between. Either way, the first step to better control your emotions is understanding them. You can't fix a car engine without knowing how all the different parts work together—emotions are the same. This week, we'll be helping you understand your emotional experiences better so that you are better equipped to cope with them.

The Nature of Emotions

Although we often talk about emotions in a pretty simplistic way (e.g., "I feel sad"), emotions are actually complex, multifaceted reactions that involve numerous systems in our minds and bodies. When we feel something, we experience physical sensations, thoughts, urges, and more. All of these are components of DBT's Model of Emotions. The Model, like emotions themselves, is complicated. Let's break it down.

Every emotion starts with a **prompting event**: a thing, event, or "trigger" that happens and causes us to feel something—the emotional experience. A prompting event can be external—something happens out in the world, like receiving a text message or someone holding your hand. A prompting event can also be internal—something happens inside you, like feeling tightness in your chest or remembering a fun vacation. Once prompted, the emotional experience itself has several different internal and external components.

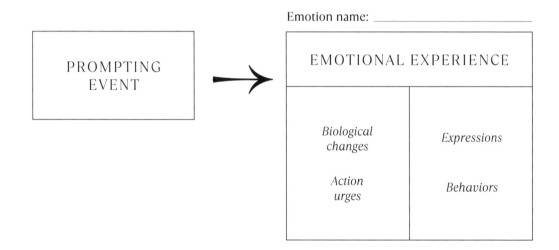

Every emotion generates internal **biological changes**. When emotions fire, neurotransmitters are released in the brain, hormones are released in the bloodstream, and your nervous system is activated. You also feel **action urges**. Emotions make you feel like doing something (or they can make you feel like *not* doing something), usually by inducing physical sensations. When you see a bear, you'll probably feel fear and notice your muscles start to tense, and then you'll probably have the action urge to run away! Action urges like this are how emotions can protect us.

Accordingly, we often act on our action urges, leading to external **expressions** and **behaviors**. When you're angry, you might yell, clench your fists, or throw something. When you're grateful, you might smile, hug someone, or say "thank you." In these ways, the biological reactions of emotional experiences are accompanied by body language, words, and actions. Finally, we label these concurrent experiences with an **emotion name**. Language is foundational to how we as humans understand our experiences, including emotions. Amazingly, just *naming* our emotions can change what we're feeling and reduce emotional pain—as Dr. Dan Siegel says about emotions, "Name it to tame it!"

Interpretations are another key feature of emotions. Sometimes, our emotions are caused by what we *think* or *believe* about prompting events, rather than the events themselves. For example, if you're waiting for a date and the person does not show up on time, what you assume will influence how you feel. If you have the thought "They must have changed their mind because I'm too ugly," you're likely to feel shame. If you have the thought "They must be stuck in traffic," you might feel some empathy for the person. Additionally, what we feel influences what we think. We *all* are more likely to think hopeless thoughts when we feel depressed, for example. Basically, there's constant interplay between our emotions and thoughts.

VULNERABILITY FACTORS

```
┌─────────────────────────┐
│                         │
│    INTERPRETATIONS      │
│                         │
└─────────────────────────┘
```

Emotion name: _____

```
┌──────────────┐              ┌────────────────────────────┐
│              │              │   EMOTIONAL EXPERIENCE     │
│  PROMPTING   │    ──────▶   ├─────────────┬──────────────┤
│   EVENT      │              │ Biological  │              │
│              │              │ changes     │ Expressions  │
└──────────────┘              │             │              │
                              │ Action      │ Behaviors    │
                              │ urges       │              │
                              └─────────────┴──────────────┘
```

This whole interaction occurs within a larger system of **vulnerability factors**, things that make you more vulnerable to certain emotional experiences. These factors can be internal or external, recent or old; maybe you're irritable and "hangry" because you missed breakfast, maybe you've had a really stressful week and the prompting event is the "straw that broke the camel's back," or maybe the prompting event reminds you of a traumatic experience you had in childhood. Vulnerability factors influence your emotions by making it more likely that you have certain types of interpretations, or by making you more biologically reactive or psychologically sensitive in a given moment.

One final important thing to note: emotions love themselves. Our emotions create **aftereffects**—consequences in ourselves or our environments.

For example, when you feel depressed, you might cancel plans with friends, which might later lead you to think about how much fun your friends are having without you, leading to loneliness, which might lead to comfort eating, leading to guilt and more depression, and the cycle continues. It is this type of repeated cycle that can keep you stuck in emotional suffering. The good news is you can change it! The first step in breaking self-perpetuating negative cycles is knowing how you feel and why you feel it.

Understanding the full Model of Emotions pictured on the next page will improve your ability to recognize your emotional cycles in real time.

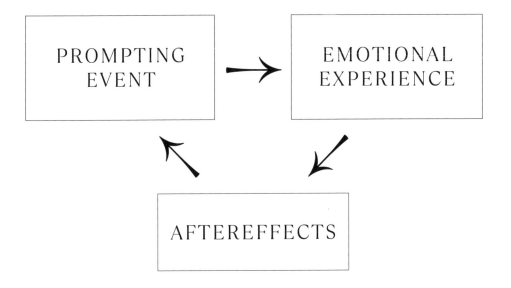

This recognition, in turn, opens the door for you to use skills, change problematic habits, and revamp your mental health.

VULNERABILITY FACTORS

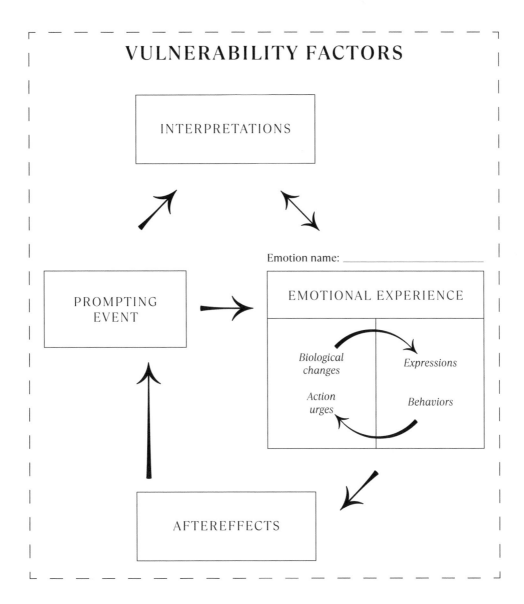

INTERPRETATIONS

Emotion name: _____

PROMPTING EVENT

EMOTIONAL EXPERIENCE

Biological changes

Expressions

Action urges

Behaviors

AFTEREFFECTS

EXERCISE: *Observing and Describing Emotions*

A fundamental skill in DBT is understanding your emotions in all their multidimensional glory by Observing and Describing them using the full Model of Emotions. Sometime during or after you feel an emotion this week, fill out the worksheet on page 58. You do not need to complete the steps in order; you can start with whatever parts of the emotion are easiest for you to observe/describe and go from there.

INSTRUCTIONS

1. On the first line, label your emotion. If you're struggling with naming your emotion, you can use the emotion words provided in the "Create Your Personal Emotion Dictionary" exercise on page 62, or use other resources for naming emotions as necessary. (See "Additional Resources" on page 207.)

2. Briefly describe the prompting event. What happened that triggered the emotion? What did you Observe? What were the who/what/where/when facts?

3. Write out the thoughts, opinions, assumptions, or beliefs you had about the prompting event.

4. Reflect on whether there were any vulnerability factors that influenced your emotion, physiological reactions, or interpretations. How were you feeling before the prompting event happened? Does the prompting event remind you of any emotional events from your past? Is there anything in your physical health that could make you more sensitive right now—think about sleep, diet, menstrual cycle, illness, pain, medications, etc.?

5. Detail how you physically felt. How did your body change while feeling the emotion? Were there any physical sensations in your face, neck, chest, stomach, limbs, or other body parts? Did you feel any tension/relief, lightness/heaviness, discomfort/pleasure, warmth/coolness?

6. Note your action urges. What did the emotion make you feel like doing, saying, or expressing?

7. Note your behaviors. What did you *actually* do or say while feeling the emotion?

8. Describe your emotional expressions. What would others have been able to see on your face and in your body language? Did you smile, frown, sneer, gasp? Did your eyebrows raise, furrow, or move? Did your eyes squint, widen, or change focus? Did your hands, head, shoulders, limbs, or body posture shift in some way? Did the tone or volume of your voice change?

9. Finally, report any aftereffects. What consequences did your emotions and your behaviors have? How did they influence your environment or other people? Did you feel any other emotions in response to the original emotion you felt? How was your body, mood, or state of mind impacted in the minutes/hours following your initial emotional reaction?

OBSERVING AND DESCRIBING AN EMOTION
WITH THE MODEL OF EMOTIONS

1. Emotion name: _____

2. Prompting event: _____

   _____

   _____

3. Interpretations: _____

   _____

   _____

4. Vulnerability factors: _____

   _____

   _____

5. Body sensations: _____

   _____

   _____

6. Action urges: _____

   _____

7. Behaviors: _____

   _____

8. Expressions: _____

   _____

9. Aftereffects: _____

   _____

EXERCISE: *Mindfulness of Current Emotions*

This exercise helps shift our focus into our bodies and allows us to just "ride the wave" of our emotion. Practice this skill when you're actively experiencing an emotion. For your first time, we recommend practicing with an emotion that's mild or moderate in intensity. You could listen to a song or watch a video that prompts you to feel an emotion of your choosing. We recommend 1–3 minutes for your first time, and then you can lengthen your practices each time.

INSTRUCTIONS

1. Take three deep breaths, close your eyes if you feel comfortable doing so, and bring your attention to the physical sensations you feel as you're experiencing your emotion. Note any action urges, and don't act on them. Simply observe what you notice in your body.

2. If you find yourself distracted by your environment or by thoughts, you could try describing the physical sensations you observe. Do you feel any tension, pain, bubbling, pleasure, burning, sweating, pounding, tightening, or tingling? Do you feel lightness or heaviness, warmth or coolness, constriction or expansion? How do different parts of your body feel?

3. Notice if the physical sensations change as you Observe or Describe them. Does your emotion appear to increase or decrease as you bring your attention to physical sensations? What happens to your action urges as you just sit with them? Can you observe your emotion like it's a wave or tide in the ocean, rising and falling, changing naturally?

continued

4. If you feel willing, practice loving your emotion. Perhaps remind yourself that this emotion will not last forever, that every person alive feels this emotion sometimes, or that emotions exist to help or protect you. Perhaps thank your body for the emotion, or thank yourself for having the courage to sit with an emotion without trying to avoid it. You can softly adjust your hands so your palms are open and facing up, put your hand over your heart, or softly stroke your own arm or face in a soothing way.

5. Whether you try Step 4 or not, just keep observing your emotion. Whenever your focus is elsewhere, bring your attention back to the emotional experience in your body. Don't try to suppress or amplify the emotion. Don't judge it. Simply feel it.

6. Finally, when you're ready, take a few more deep breaths to end the exercise.

It's easy to get caught up in our heads when we're emotional; when we're anxious, we often worry about how everything could go wrong, and when we're sad, we often ruminate about how everything *is* wrong. Focusing on our thoughts, however, leaves us vulnerable to creating more emotional suffering. One of the most effective ways to overcome this thinking trap is to tap into the physical sensations of our emotions.

That being said, we know emotions can be painful. They may even feel dangerous, particularly if you struggle with panic attacks or if you engage in harmful behaviors when you are very upset. Emotions themselves cannot hurt us, however. In their natural state, emotions are short term, usually lasting no more than two minutes unless we strengthen them with emotional thinking. Trying to avoid or suppress our emotions also keeps them around longer, just buried deeper in our brains or bodies.

Practicing Mindfulness of Current Emotions by focusing on physical sensations can teach us how to sit with emotions without overthinking, without acting impulsively, and without becoming overwhelmed. It can remind us that emotions can't hurt us, we are not our emotions, and emotions aren't wrong or bad. *Emotions just are.* This skill can be really tough, we know. So, if needed, continue to limit your initial practices to lower-intensity emotions, to seconds at a time, or to specific body parts rather than your whole body. With more practice, your comfort with and control of your emotions will increase.

EXERCISE: *Create Your Personal Emotion Dictionary*

For this final exercise, you'll create your own "emotion dictionary" by reflecting on how *you* feel specific emotions. By identifying patterns in the way that you have experienced certain emotions in the past, you will be able to more easily recognize and name them when you feel them in the future. This exercise could take some time to complete—feel free to complete it in pieces across this week or future weeks.

INSTRUCTIONS

1. Review the eight emotions on pages 64 to 67. For each emotion, we've also provided other emotion labels that are related to the main emotion listed. If you aren't sure what a word means, we encourage you to look it up.

2. For each emotion, identify at least one time in your life when you have previously felt that emotion and briefly describe it. Please choose a time you can easily recall your emotional experience, even if you don't remember it perfectly—a more recent memory might be easiest. (We included common types of prompting events for each of the eight emotions to help guide you, but they are not the only possibilities.) When completing the following steps, you can reflect on this specific emotional experience, or on your experience generally, whenever you feel this emotion.

3. Next, think about the action urge you felt when experiencing that emotion. What did the emotion make you feel like doing? What has that emotion made you feel like doing at other times you've felt it? We included common action urges for each emotion. If any of the suggested action urges resonate with your experiences, circle them; write your specific action urges into the provided space.

4. Finally, reflect on what else you can observe and describe about your experience when feeling the emotion, using the questions from the exercise "Observing and Describing Emotions" on page 58. Are there certain physical sensations, expressions, behaviors, or interpretations that normally accompany this emotion for you? Is there anything else about experiencing this emotion that stands out for you—even something not captured by the DBT Model of Emotions? For example, someone might write the following for their experience of sadness: "physically tired, heaviness, thinking about all of the issues wrong with the world, just wanting to sleep, seeing blue or darkness, desire to be in the dark and listen to sad music or read philosophy."

Naming our emotions can give us self-confidence and power, but it can be very difficult. It requires us to be aware of our emotions and to be knowledgeable about various emotional words and experiences— something that we're (usually) not taught in school, and often not taught at all! Practicing labeling and describing our emotions can help us improve. The more specific we can get about how we're feeling, the better we can understand ourselves and the better we can communicate our needs to others. Although there are many more emotion words than the ones we've included here, this exercise is a place to start. We've included some resources for growing your emotional vocabulary in the "Additional Resources" section on page 207.

continued

Emotion: Sadness	Emotion: Disgust
hurt, depressed, disappointed, lonely	*repulsed, grossed out, contempt, hate*

TIME I'VE FELT SAD: _____

_____

_____

COMMON PROMPTING EVENTS: losing someone or something you care about; things not working out how you wanted; being excluded or isolated; hearing about other people's grief or problems; distressing news

ACTION URGES: stop and cry, seek comfort, rest and slow down, curl up, isolate

_____

_____

WHAT DOES SADNESS FEEL LIKE FOR ME?

_____

_____

_____

_____

_____

_____

_____

_____

TIME I'VE FELT DISGUSTED: _____

_____

_____

COMMON PROMPTING EVENTS: you're physically near something that could make you sick; someone or something is morally repellent to you

ACTION URGES: recoil, get away from, remove or clean up, change or avoid someone, vomit, be rude or cold toward someone, wash/clean

_____

_____

WHAT DOES DISGUST FEEL LIKE FOR ME?

_____

_____

_____

_____

_____

_____

_____

_____

| **Emotion: Happiness** | **Emotion: Fear** |
| *joyful, content, delighted, enthusiastic* | *anxious, dread, ill at ease, panicked* |

TIME I'VE FELT HAPPY: _____

_____

_____

COMMON PROMPTING EVENTS: getting something you want; achieving something you've worked for; being praised/credited/ loved/accepted; being part of a group; hearing good news for yourself or someone you care for; feeling pleasure

ACTION URGES: smile, share joy with others, focus on positive things, take up space

_____

_____

WHAT DOES HAPPINESS FEEL LIKE FOR ME?

_____

_____

_____

_____

_____

_____

_____

TIME I'VE FELT AFRAID: _____

_____

_____

COMMON PROMPTING EVENTS: the life, health, or well-being of you or someone you care about is in danger; being in a situation that reminds you of a time you've been threatened/hurt before; being alone or in the dark, unknown, or unfamiliar

ACTION URGES: avoid what you fear, run away, escape, freeze up/shut down, hide

_____

_____

WHAT DOES FEAR FEEL LIKE FOR ME?

_____

_____

_____

_____

_____

_____

_____

Emotion: Anger	Emotion: Love
frustrated, enraged, indignant, irritated	*warm, affectionate, limerent, caring*

TIME I'VE FELT ANGRY: _____

_____

_____

COMMON PROMPTING EVENTS: you or someone who matters to you are attacked, threatened, or disrespected; you're kept from getting something you want or from reaching a goal; things aren't the way you want them to be in the world (e.g., social injustice)

ACTION URGES: fight or attack, be aggressive, criticize, intimidate, protect or defend, work toward change

_____

_____

WHAT DOES ANGER FEEL LIKE FOR ME?

_____

_____

_____

_____

_____

_____

TIME I'VE FELT LOVE: _____

_____

_____

COMMON PROMPTING EVENTS: someone/ something provides things you want, need, or value; being with someone you have fun with, have great communication with, or share a special connection with (e.g., biological, emotional, cultural); physical attraction

ACTION URGES: touch or be near the thing or person you love, fantasize or daydream about the person or thing you love

_____

_____

WHAT DOES LOVE FEEL LIKE FOR ME?

_____

_____

_____

_____

_____

_____

Emotion: Guilt	**Emotion: Shame**
remorse, regret, sorry	*embarrassed, mortified, self-conscious*

TIME I'VE FELT GUILTY:_____

_____

_____

COMMON PROMPTING EVENTS: behaving, speaking, or thinking in a way that goes against your values or morals; harming someone else or yourself; failing to keep a commitment you made

ACTION URGES: apologize, acknowledge your wrongdoing, repair or work to correct, change your behavior/thinking

_____

_____

WHAT DOES GUILT FEEL LIKE FOR ME?

_____

_____

_____

_____

_____

_____

_____

TIME I'VE FELT ASHAMED: _____

_____

_____

COMMON PROMPTING EVENTS: being rejected, criticized, stigmatized, invalidated, or made fun of; believing you are bad or not living up to some standard; having a private part of yourself made public

ACTION URGES: hide and withdraw/isolate, punish yourself, hide your "transgressions" or "negative" features

_____

_____

WHAT DOES SHAME FEEL LIKE FOR ME?

_____

_____

_____

_____

_____

_____

_____

Work Through Emotional Blocks

WEEK 4

Often people come to DBT because they're feeling emotionally stuck and looking for ways to get out of painful emotional loops. If that describes you, then you're going to like the next two chapters! This week, we'll be teaching you two DBT skills specific to reducing emotions that you don't want to feel: Checking the Facts and Opposite Action. Though they both can be tough to use and challenging to master, they are two of the most powerful skills we have to offer you.

The Difference Between Thoughts and Facts

Last week, we introduced the idea that thoughts are one part of our emotional experience. What we think about a prompting event can change how we feel about it, *and* how we feel can change what we're thinking. For example, if you take a selfie after getting a new haircut and send it to your friend, and she doesn't say anything, you may feel sadness if you believe she's not responding because she doesn't like your hair. Your sadness, in turn, may then lead you to have more judgmental thoughts like "it looks stupid" that will then lead you to feel shame or regret.

What would it mean, however, if your friend didn't respond because she missed the notification on her phone? If she texts you an hour later saying she loves it, you'll probably feel happy, relieved, or excited. Turns out that you experienced a whole ton of emotional suffering for no reason because you got stuck treating your initial thoughts like they were facts!

Reacting to inaccurate beliefs can also cause us *more* emotional pain by creating new problems. In the haircut example, if in your distress you angrily text her "you never support me!" then you're likely to anger or hurt your friend, causing a conflict that might not have happened if instead you waited for her to text back. Acting as if our thoughts are facts can get us into trouble in a lot of ways.

We are *not* saying that your thoughts are always wrong. Sometimes, our emotions are a natural response to the prompting events, and our related thoughts may be accurate. At other times, however, the majority (or entirety!) of our emotional pain comes from our interpretations about what happened, rather than what actually happened. Distinguishing between our thoughts and the facts can be incredibly helpful in decreasing our emotional suffering.

The DBT skill of Checking the Facts provides a specific framework for examining the accuracy of our interpretations in various ways. It prompts us to imagine as many different perspectives as we can. It also offers a way to respond more effectively to the black-and-white or catastrophic thoughts we may have when feeling negative emotions (e.g., beliefs like "everything is hopeless," "my life is going to fall apart," or "they're going to leave me"). By increasing our ability to think more flexibly and accurately, Checking the Facts helps us regulate our emotions. You will learn these specific techniques and have a chance to practice during this week's exercises.

Change How You're Acting to Change How You Feel

As helpful as Checking the Facts can be for changing painful emotions, it's often not enough. Sometimes your initial interpretations are accurate, and your emotion fits the facts; in that case, you need Problem Solving, a skill we'll learn next week. In other situations, you may never find out whether your interpretations are right. Or, you may not actually feel any better despite determining that your thoughts are inaccurate. In these cases, what are you supposed to do?

Enter: Opposite Action. Last week, we learned that emotions cause us to have action urges—impulses to do or say things associated with that emotion. We also highlighted how emotions love themselves and often make us behave in ways that keep them around. Opposite Action is *acting opposite* to an emotion's action urges, which changes how you feel by interrupting the emotion's self-loving cycle.

What does this look like? Let's say you struggle with social anxiety, and your friend invites you to a group dinner where there will be people you don't know. When the time of the dinner comes around, you feel intense anxiety and have urges to cancel last minute. Acting opposite is going to the dinner! But that's not quite enough. If you go to the dinner but then stay silent, avoid eye contact, worry about how everyone is perceiving you, and leave early, you're still stuck in a lot of the features of anxiety that you learned about in the Model of Emotions last week (e.g., thoughts, behaviors, expressions). Therefore, you're likely to leave the dinner feeling just as anxious as at the start of the night—and possibly a bit worse.

To act opposite in a way that will decrease your emotion, you must act opposite *all the way* to every part of the Model, and you often need to repeat it over and over. You need to go to the dinner, make eye contact, focus on what people are saying (rather than your anxious thoughts), tell a story, smile, and stay until the end. If you still feel some anxiety at the start of the night, that makes sense, but it's likely to decrease over the course of the night. Even if it doesn't go away completely, you'll hopefully leave the dinner having experienced some happiness and connection, perhaps having made a new friend, and feeling more confident for the next dinner invitation.

Below are a few more examples of Opposite Action. We hope these will help you figure out how you might use Opposite Action in your life.

EMOTION: Anxiety

EXAMPLE WAYS TO ACT OPPOSITE: approach (rather than avoid), do what you're afraid of doing, act confident, breathe slowly and deeply, talk animatedly

EMOTION: Sadness

EXAMPLE WAYS TO ACT OPPOSITE: spend time with people (rather than isolate), do more pleasurable or meaningful activities (rather than avoid them), schedule more activities, increase movement or act excited, keep your body posture upright, practice gratitude

EMOTION: Anger

EXAMPLE WAYS TO ACT OPPOSITE: do something nice for someone (rather than attack them), walk away or take a break (rather than fight), breathe slowly and deeply, relax your body, lower your voice

EMOTION: Shame

EXAMPLE WAYS TO ACT OPPOSITE: make your behaviors/characteristics public (rather than hide them), share your internal experiences with other people, connect with people who share your interests/identities, don't apologize for things that don't go against your morals, act confident, make eye contact, ask for things you want or say no clearly, do kind things for yourself, practice self-compassion

---

Opposite Action is so effective that there are psychotherapies entirely based on acting opposite. Exposure therapy, which involves approaching things you're scared of (when you desperately want to avoid them), is one of the most effective treatments for anxiety disorders. Behavioral Activation, which involves engaging in pleasurable and meaningful activities (when you don't feel like it), is one of the most effective therapies for depression. Basically, Opposite Action is a way to "fake it till you make it" that actually works!

There are two scenarios in which Opposite Action is the skill to use in order to decrease unwanted emotion. First, use Opposite Action when your emotion does not fit the facts (or its intensity does not fit the facts). For example, if you're in love with your ex who was abusive toward you, it would be effective to act opposite to love-inspired urges to get back together with them, as love would not fit the facts in that situation. Second, use Opposite Action when it is not effective for you to act on your emotion. For example, if you're feeling melancholic and have urges to not go into work for the third day in a row, it's probably not helpful for you to act on that urge and miss work again (even if your sadness fits the facts).

If all of this sounds tough, that's because it can be! Opposite Action is a challenging skill. It also sometimes needs repetition or time in order to work. In our previous social anxiety example, you may have to attend two or 10 dinner parties before the anxiety goes down or goes away. The good news is that it's also a really, really effective skill and, like everything, it gets easier with practice.

EXERCISE: *Differentiating Between Thoughts and Facts*

Noticing the difference between the facts and our thoughts is essential for improving emotional well-being. One of the most effective ways to practice this skill is to reflect on recent emotional experiences and differentiate between the prompting event itself and your interpretations of the event.

INSTRUCTIONS

1. Think about three times in the past week that you felt an emotion, and complete the table on page 74 for each experience.

2. In the first column, briefly describe the prompting event for the emotion. What happened right before you felt what you felt? Write only the who/what/where/when information that you directly observed with your own senses.

3. In the second column, write your interpretations of the prompting event. What did you believe about the facts? Did you make any assumptions about anything? What thoughts did you have?

4. In the third column, label your emotion(s). What did you feel in response to the prompting event and your interpretations? (Note: this column will be one-word answers only! If you notice you're using phrases or sentences, it's likely you're actually describing a thought rather than an emotion. Your emotion dictionary from last week can help.)

You may find it interesting to note whether your emotion (or its intensity) changes at all when you distinguish between the facts of what happened and your interpretations of those facts!

continued

PROMPTING EVENT	INTERPRETATIONS/ THOUGHTS	EMOTION(S)
I showed my new haircut to my friend and she didn't say anything about it.	*She hates it.* *It's a bad haircut.* *I look stupid.*	*sadness, regret, shame*

EXERCISE: *Checking the Facts*

In this exercise you will practice Checking the Facts using the worksheet on page 77. Choose a time when you're feeling an emotion at a moderate level—something intense enough to have some meat to it, but not too intense that you feel overwhelmed.

INSTRUCTIONS

Fill out the worksheet on page 77 as you complete the following steps.

1. First, identify your emotion. What exactly are you feeling? Use the skills you practiced last week to help you recognize and label your emotional experience.

2. Describe the prompting event and your interpretations separately, like you did in the previous exercise. Differentiate between *what you directly observed* through your senses (i.e., the objective facts of the situation) and *what you thought* about what you observed.

3. Notice if your interpretations are "adding on" anything to the prompting event. Might a "fly on the wall" disagree with how you described the situation? Are there other ways to look at this situation? Write down as many perspectives and interpretations as you can think of, even if you feel confident in your initial interpretation. Using Wise Mind, circle the interpretation that is most likely to be true. (Sometimes it will be your original thought, sometimes not.)

continued

4. Notice if you're viewing the prompting event as a "threat," expecting that it will lead to painful or unwanted consequences. What are you most worried might happen because of it? How likely is this outcome? Are there other possible outcomes? Write down all the outcomes you can imagine. Using Wise Mind, circle the one that is most likely.

5. Allow yourself to truly answer any "what if" worry thoughts. *What if* the worst possible outcome does happen? *What if* your worries come true? What could you actually do in case of the catastrophe? How could you problem solve? Who or what could you lean on for support? Would it be as bad as your current emotion wants you to believe it to be? Note the worst-case scenario, and then briefly write out your best coping plan.

6. Finally, considering all the above steps you've taken to explore your thoughts, ask yourself in Wise Mind: "Did my initial emotion, identified in Step 1, fit the facts? Was it justified by the facts?" In DBT, an emotion is *justified* only when it fits the reality of the situation based on facts alone, separate from interpretations. This is different from an emotion being *valid*; if you're feeling something, then it makes sense you're feeling it and the emotion *is* valid. When determining whether an emotion fits the facts, it's also important to consider the intensity or duration of the emotion relative to the prompting event.

7. If you're unsure whether your emotion is justified by the facts, take a break and repeat Steps 3–5, check out the "common prompting events" in the emotion dictionary from last week, ask friends for their opinions, or research whether your interpretations or predictions are accurate.

Checking the Facts can be difficult. No one can think clearly when they're 10-out-of-10 upset—sometimes you have to use Distress Tolerance skills (which we're going to cover in Weeks 7–9) before using this skill. It's also hard to Check the Facts when you're emotionally vulnerable. But the more you practice Checking the Facts, the easier it will become, whatever your mood.

CHECKING THE FACTS WORKSHEET

1. Emotion name: _____

2. Prompting event: _____
   _____

3. Initial interpretations: _____
   _____
   _____

   Other possible interpretations: _____
   _____
   _____

4. The threat I'm worried about: _____
   _____

   Other possible outcomes: _____
   _____
   _____

5. The catastrophe I'm worried about: _____
   _____

   What I could actually do to cope: _____
   _____
   _____
   _____
   _____
   _____

6. Does my emotion fit the facts? (circle one)
   YES   NOT AT ALL   NOT THE INTENSITY   NOT SURE

EXERCISE: *Opposite Action*

We recommend that you practice acting opposite at least twice this week to an emotion that either doesn't fit the facts or isn't effective for you to act on. For at least one practice, write about your experience using the worksheet on page 80. Reflecting on your Opposite Action experience will help you learn from your practice so you can act opposite more easily and effectively in the future.

INSTRUCTIONS

1. Identify the emotion you want to change. What exactly are you feeling? Use the skills you practiced last week to help you recognize and label your emotional experience.

2. Check the Facts. Is your emotion justified (rather than just being valid)? Does your emotion (and its intensity or duration) fit the facts? If needed, use the Checking the Facts worksheet on page 77!

3. Identify your action urges. What does your emotion make you feel like saying, doing, or expressing? Does your body feel pressured to act/respond in a specific way? Refer to your emotion dictionary for action urges you could be feeling in response to the emotion.

4. Check effectiveness. Practice Wise Mind and ask: Would following through on my action urges be effective? Would acting the way the emotion wants me to act cause me any problems? Would it help me?

5. Confirm that Opposite Action is the skill to use. Did you determine that the emotion you're feeling is either unjustified, ineffective, or both? If so, continue! If not, either acting on the emotion or Problem Solving (next week's skill!) are likely the best options.

6. Identify the essential Opposite Actions. Think about the action urges you described in Step 3; what is the *opposite* of acting on your emotion? What would you do or not do?

7. Identify the all-the-way Opposite Actions. How can you change your body posture, face, voice tone? How could you change or refocus your thoughts? (Rather than just forcing untrue "happy thoughts" in response to sadness, for example, you could work to actively reframe your perspective, focus on different aspects of things around you, or fill your mind with other unrelated thoughts or sensations.) How can you continue to act opposite fully, even if the unwanted emotion continues?

8. Finally, act opposite! Take the first step, and then keep acting opposite over and over until your unwanted emotion diminishes or disappears.

It is especially helpful to proactively plan and schedule ways to practice Opposite Action for any specific emotions that you consistently struggle with and find more challenging. For example, for social anxiety, you could go out of your way to try to meet new people, rather than wait for your friend to invite you to a dinner. When we consistently have trouble managing a specific emotion, often it is because of how trapped we become in the emotion's self-loving cycle—the emotion causes us to act in ways that feed and maintain it, potentially in ways that we might not even realize. Though it is very hard to practice, there's no skill quite as powerful as Opposite Action in getting us "unstuck" from this cyclical emotional suffering.

OPPOSITE ACTION WORKSHEET

1. What was I feeling at first? _____

2. What was the prompting event? _____

3. Did my emotion fit the facts? (circle one)

   YES   NOT AT ALL   NOT THE INTENSITY   NOT SURE

4. Why or why not? _____

   _____

5. What were my action urges? _____

   _____

6. Would acting on my action urges have been effective? (circle one)

   YES   NO

7. Why or why not? _____

   _____

8. What did I do to act opposite? _____

   _____

9. Did my emotion change? (circle one)

   A LITTLE   A LOT   NO

10. What were the aftereffects to my mind, mood, body, or environment? _____

    _____

11. Is there any way I could've acted opposite more *all the way*? How? _____

    _____

12. What would be most effective in a similar situation next time? _____

    _____

Decrease Stressors to Decrease Stress

WEEK 5

Last week, you learned skills that can be helpful when you experience emotions that don't fit the facts or that aren't effective for you to act on. Sometimes our emotions do fit the facts, though—the situation itself is the problem, not our interpretation! For example, if you are put on probation at work and you're afraid you will lose your job, the problem is your job situation, and the most effective way to decrease your anxiety is to improve your job performance (or perhaps to find another job).

In other words, in order to regulate your emotions in situations in which your emotions fit the facts, the most effective thing to do is often to change the situation—that is when the Problem Solving skills are useful.

Problems? Sorry, I Don't Have Any

We all face challenges, whether in our relationships, our finances, our professional or academic lives, or our physical or emotional health. In DBT, we consider all of these things that cause justified painful emotions to be problems. For this reason, it is virtually impossible to regulate our emotions or build a satisfying, fulfilling Life Worth Living without Problem Solving skills.

Problem Solving skills can also be a helpful way to change impulsive, out-of-control, or otherwise unwanted behaviors. When someone struggles to regulate their behavior, the behavior itself is often viewed as "the Problem." For example, if someone impulsively spends a lot of money in response to anxiety, the shopping spree is likely to be treated as the Problem—and of course, it is *a* problem! When we use Problem Solving skills, though, we view the person's spending as an ineffective "solution" to whatever problem prompted their anxiety. Reframing the unwanted behavior this way and focusing on solving the initial problem that caused the anxiety will decrease the likelihood of both future anxiety and future shopping sprees—win-win!

Though problems are a fact of life, many people fail to recognize when there is something that needs solving—or don't acknowledge it until it has built up and become much harder to solve. Even when someone is aware of an issue, a variety of factors can interfere with addressing it effectively. Some people oversimplify problems or underestimate the difficulty of addressing the situation. Others treat problems as threats that need to be avoided rather than challenges to be met. The Problem Solving skills address each of these issues in order to set you up for success.

Defining the Problem

Problem Solving involves several steps, each of which protect you against one of several factors that can interfere with effectively solving the problem you're facing. The very first step is to define the problem. Although this may sound obvious, often people react to a situation without actually observing and describing what about it is problematic for them. For example, let's say Elliot wants to use his Problem Solving skills because he is feeling angry at

Kiki after she didn't return his calls. He might be angry because he thinks Kiki doesn't want to talk to him or because he couldn't work on a shared project until they discussed some details. Clarifying what about the situation is problematic can lead to very different solutions. Additionally, accurately describing the problem is necessary if you want to communicate about it effectively.

Once you have defined the problem, pause and use your Check the Facts skills to ensure that you are describing the problem accurately. This step is like coming to a stop sign in the road; you must "look both ways" and make sure you are responding to the facts rather than to your thoughts or interpretations before proceeding with Problem Solving. To return to our example, if Elliot Checks the Facts and determines that he truly cannot work on the project until he speaks to Kiki, he should move forward with Problem Solving. If he realizes that he is angry because of the interpretation that Kiki doesn't want to talk to him, however, Checking the Facts will help him realize that this is actually an assumption and not necessarily a fact. He would not proceed with Problem Solving until he determines what, if anything, is actually problematic about the situation.

Now that you are clear on what problem you want to solve, it is time to identify your goal in this situation. The question at this stage is what would need to happen for your unwanted emotions to change or decrease—in other words, for you to feel satisfied that the problem has been addressed. In our example, Elliot may identify his goal as being able to continue working on the shared project; it could be that he wants an agreed-upon plan to ensure that this doesn't happen again; or he might simply want an apology. This is an important step because if you aren't clear on your goal, you will be less likely to solve the problem in a way that leaves you feeling satisfied.

Brainstorming and Choosing a Solution

Once you have identified your goal, the challenge is determining how to achieve it! Problem Solving often goes awry at this step. People tend to come up with one solution and either run with it if it sounds good or immediately dismiss it if they see a potential pitfall. The problem is that the first idea may not be the most effective one, even if it looks like a solid option; on the other hand, it could be the best option, even if it's not perfect.

Instead, the thing to do here is to brainstorm as many options as you can for how to achieve your goal, and to suspend your judgment of the options—no matter how absurd they may seem—until you can't think of any other possibilities. The more potential solutions you generate, the more likely it is that you will come up with an effective solution to your problem. Returning to our example, let's say Elliot decided his goal was to continue working on the shared project. His brainstorming might include the following: tell Kiki that he wants to talk so he can continue working, deliberately be late with his portion of the project so she learns her lesson, try to get Kiki to be more responsive by buying her cookies every time she replies to him, and so on.

Once you have written down as many ideas as you can, the next step is to select the solution (or solutions) to implement. There are two factors to consider: How likely is each option to work in achieving your goal, and how feasible is it?

It may help to start with a process of elimination; some ideas are obviously unrealistic, and others will be worth a closer look. After narrowing down your list to the top few options, you can rank-order them based on the fit with your goal and their feasibility. Complete a pros and cons list of the top remaining options (using the format we will introduce in Week 7); or access your Wise Mind. These strategies will help you identify which solution is most likely to be effective.

Take Action!

All the previous steps lead to this—it's time to implement your solution! If your solution is complex or you find yourself feeling anxious, break it down into small steps. This way, you can focus on just the one step in front of you, which often feels more manageable. If other roadblocks appear, think about whether additional skills (e.g., Opposite Action) might be helpful.

Once you have implemented your solution, the final step is to evaluate the outcome: Did the solution work? Was your goal achieved? If so, be mindful of your success and celebrate it! If your goal wasn't achieved, or if the solution was only partially effective, consider implementing another one of the solutions you generated.

Problem Solving: Quick Reference

You can use this quick reference as a resource any time you want to utilize your Problem Solving skills.

STEP 1: Define the problem. What is problematic about this situation? Check the Facts to be sure you are responding to the facts of the situation.

STEP 2: Identify your goal. What needs to happen or change for you to be satisfied?

STEP 3: Brainstorm! Come up with as many solutions as you can, and remember to suspend your judgment and critical thinking for this step.

STEP 4: Choose a solution. Narrow down your options using process of elimination, Wise Mind, and pros and cons, and select the solution you think is feasible and most likely to achieve your goal.

STEP 5: Implement your solution. If necessary, break it down into small, manageable steps.

STEP 6: Evaluate the outcome, defining success based on whether your goal was achieved. If so, celebrate! If not, consider another one of the solutions you brainstormed. Apply your Problem Solving skills again to address any new or additional problems.

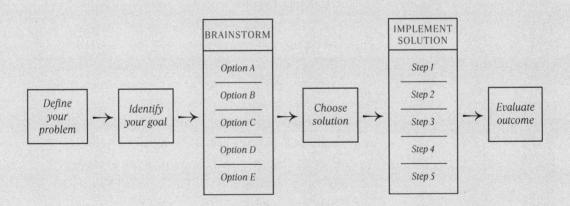

EXERCISE: *Identify Opportunities for Problem Solving*

We often fail to recognize when there is a problem that needs solving, or avoid facing it until it has become too big to ignore. In this exercise, you will consider some of the situations in your own life in which Problem Solving skills could be helpful. Please be sure to read all the instructions before you begin to write!

INSTRUCTIONS

1. On the next page, list any and all problems in your life. These can include one-off problems (e.g., an argument with a friend, a job interview) or recurring/ongoing problems (e.g., relationship issues, social anxiety, financial stress). It can be helpful to think about what situations bring up painful emotions or lead to problematic behaviors, as these are often the ones in which we need Problem Solving skills the most.

2. In listing each problem, describe just the facts as nonjudgmentally as possible. Don't judge problems as too big or too small to include, or leave anything out because you think it "shouldn't" be a problem for you. If you need more space than provided here, please continue on a separate piece of paper.

Thinking about the problems in our lives almost always brings up painful emotions, and you may feel tempted to procrastinate, stop writing, or rush through this exercise. If this is the case, try to create your list again using your new Opposite Action skills (e.g., take your time, be thorough, breathe slowly and deeply, and relax any tension you notice in your body and your facial muscles). While this process may be difficult in the short term, it will almost certainly be more effective for you in the long term than avoidance.

MY PROBLEM LIST

EXERCISE: *Identifying Your Goals*

A common mistake is to confuse goals with solutions. A goal is an outcome you want in a situation—for example, an apology from a friend or a raise at work. Solutions, on the other hand, are the methods you use to try to bring about that outcome. In this exercise, you will practice identifying goals for a few of the problems you listed in the previous exercise. You will practice generating solutions in the next exercise.

INSTRUCTIONS

1. Refer to the Problem List you created in the previous exercise. Choose a few problems that you would like to focus on solving now, and list these in the table on the next page. We recommend starting with problems that feel more manageable for the purpose of this practice exercise, rather than the biggest problems in your life.

2. Next, identify your goal for each of the problems you have identified. What would need to change or happen in this situation for you to feel better? What is the outcome you want? Be as specific as possible.

3. Check your work! Make sure the goals you have identified are realistic, and focus on things that you can work toward in the short term. If you have a longer-term goal in mind, consider intermediate goals along the path to that longer-term goal. For example, if your long-term goal is to graduate from college with honors and you are only a first-year student, you might set the goal of achieving certain grades this semester.

4. Ask yourself: If I achieve this goal, will I think I made progress on this problem? Will it lead to any emotional change? If the answer is no, consider whether you might actually have a different goal.

PROBLEM	GOAL

Some of your problems may seem impossible to solve. Continue practicing Opposite Action as needed, and don't succumb to any urges to avoid thinking about your goals in these situations. Focus on identifying realistic, achievable goals; don't dismiss goals that are actually possible, and don't ignore the truth of the challenges you face. If you find yourself unable to identify a goal for any given problem, consider whether you are thinking in all-or-nothing terms. Is there an outcome that might represent progress, even if the problem wouldn't be completely solved?

EXERCISE: *Brainstorming*

Brainstorming is harder than it sounds! In this exercise, you will practice brainstorming in the context of one of your personal goals. As always, for the purpose of learning a new skill, it is most effective to practice at a manageable level of difficulty. When choosing a goal for this exercise, pick one that is mildly to moderately challenging, rather than the biggest or most complex goal on your list.

INSTRUCTIONS

1. Refer to the goals you identified in the previous exercise, and choose a moderately challenging one that you would like to work on now.

2. Brainstorm as many ideas as possible for how to achieve this goal and write them down in the table on the next page. Don't evaluate or dismiss any options as they come to you—write *everything* down! Continue on a separate piece of paper if necessary.

3. If you find yourself thinking of solutions that all fall into the same general approach, do your best to think outside that box. For example, if your goal is to get a new job and your solutions are all job-searching websites (e.g., "I can search on monster.com, indeed.com, simplyhired.com"), try to think of other ways that people find jobs (e.g., you can make cold calls to companies or ask friends in the industry if they know of anyone hiring). If you hit a wall and can't think of many ideas, ask someone you trust for suggestions or search the internet for additional options.

4. Keep going until you can't think of any more options, or until you are confident that you have thought of everything with a reasonable chance of success.

5. Once you're done brainstorming, choose which solution to implement using process of elimination, Wise Mind, and pros and cons. Consider how effective each solution would be in achieving your goal, and how feasible each would be to implement. Circle your chosen solution.

6. If necessary, break your solution down into small, manageable steps. Write down the first step you will take.

GOAL I WOULD LIKE TO ACHIEVE	
Potential solutions for my goal	
First step toward my chosen solution	

For many people, suspending critical thinking is the most difficult part of brainstorming. Notice if you start evaluating the ideas you generate, and bring your attention back to just coming up with more ideas. You may also find it helpful to deliberately think of some options that are clearly ineffective or ridiculous as a way to get your brain out of critical thinking mode!

Build Emotional Resilience

WEEK 6

Much of what we have discussed in this module has focused on what you can do to cope with unwanted emotions once they arise. You know what they say, though: "An ounce of prevention is worth a pound of cure." This week, you will learn several strategies you can use to protect yourself from Emotion Mind by increasing feelings of joy, fulfillment, and accomplishment. Keep in mind, experiencing emotions is part of being human; the goal is not to avoid experiencing painful emotions entirely! Instead, these skills will help decrease how often you experience unwanted or unhelpful emotions, how long they last, and how intense they are.

Positive Emotions: Your Buffer Against Emotion Mind

When we think about taking care of our physical health, we often consider two components: what to do when something is going wrong or not working (for example, see a doctor, get physical therapy, or have surgery), and what to do to protect our health and well-being even when nothing is "wrong" (for example, exercise, eat healthy, and take your vitamins). When it comes to your emotional health, the same is true. The previous two weeks focused on what you can do to recover or cope when unwanted emotions arise. This week, we will introduce two skills you can use to protect yourself against these emotions arising in the first place: Accumulating Positive Emotions and Building Mastery.

At the most basic level, the idea behind these two strategies is quite simple: it is hard to feel satisfied with your life if you don't consistently experience positive events and emotions! Additionally, increasing pleasant events is necessary to protect against painful emotions. For example, consider how you would be affected by a breakup in the following two scenarios: in scenario #1, you have a successful career, colleagues that you love, and supportive friends and family. In scenario #2, you hate your job, find your colleagues standoffish, and have limited social support. The breakup will undoubtedly be painful in either scenario, but it will presumably be much harder to cope with in scenario #2. When we don't experience enough positive emotions in our lives, we're more vulnerable to the effects of distressing events; think of Accumulating Positive Events and Building Mastery as ways of creating a buffer against those events.

There are three types of activities that we will discuss in this chapter: those that create positive emotions in the short term, those that create positive emotions in the long term, and those that create feelings of mastery.

Accumulate Positive Emotions in the Short Term

Accumulating Positive Emotions in the Short Term is about doing things that feel good right now, or "pleasant events." The goal is to engage in at least one pleasant event every day that brings up feelings like joy, pleasure, fun, excitement, pride, or love, just to name a few. When you speak to a friend, spend time with your dog, or engage in a hobby, you are practicing Accumulating Positive Emotions. Some people dismiss these types of experiences because the emotions are short lived, or because these activities don't feel meaningful—don't fall into this trap! Even "small" things can still have a big impact, especially when done consistently.

When we discuss this skill with our clients, one of the most common things we hear is that despite their best efforts to plan and engage in pleasant events, they are still not experiencing positive emotions. If you find this to be the case, consider whether you are fully present and mindfully participating during these events. Often we engage in an activity that has the potential to be enjoyable or rewarding, but we don't actually experience any positive emotions because we aren't being mindful of them.

It's like the last day of vacation—your body may be relaxing on the beach but if your brain is already back at work, thinking about tomorrow, you're not going to enjoy the beach nearly as much! The same is true if you are multitasking—for example, doing something on your phone while you are with friends. To get the most out of pleasant events, use your mindfulness skills such as Participating One-Mindfully and Nonjudgmentally to shift your focus away from whatever thoughts or distractions are holding your attention and back to what you are doing in the present moment.

Accumulate Positive Emotions in the Long Term

Whereas Accumulating Positive Emotions in the Short Term is all about what can make you feel different immediately, Accumulating Positive Emotions in the Long Term is about working toward long-term goals and living life in a way that is consistent with your values. This often increases our sense of meaning, fulfillment, and satisfaction over time. Additionally, behaving based on your goals and values often results in a positive feedback loop in which positive events are more likely to continue occurring in the long term.

Even just identifying your values can be difficult, and many people aren't clear on the difference between their values and their goals. Think of values as the things that you consider most important, or guiding principles in your life (e.g., "make the world a better place," "be your own person," or "treat others as I want to be treated."). You can search for "values inventory," "values list," or similar terms on the internet to find ideas and examples of common values. Whereas you can achieve a goal and move on from it, you don't "achieve" a value; you aim to continue living in a way that is consistent with it. For example, if you have the value of being physically healthy, there is no point at which you would say, "I'm healthy and in great shape. I'm done taking care of my physical health now!" You could, however, say that you have achieved the goal of running a seven-minute mile. As you can see from this example, values and goals are connected. By setting and working toward goals that are related to your values, you can increase the experience of life feeling meaningful, fulfilling, and "worth living."

You may have noticed that Accumulating Positive Emotions in the Long Term may *not* feel very enjoyable in the short term! Training for that seven-minute mile might bring up sadness, shame, or frustration along the way, not to mention physical pain and fatigue—especially early in the process. Think of these short-term challenges as an investment in your emotional well-being. Over time, you will begin to see the results you want in your life and your relationships, and the positive emotions will follow.

Build Mastery

The third and final skill this week is Building Mastery, which means doing things that give you a feeling of capability, accomplishment, or pride. These activities are usually ones in which you are developing a skill or doing something that you find challenging—for example, learning to play a musical instrument or DIYing something in your home. Another great example is practicing and developing your DBT skills! By consistently engaging in these types of activities, your self-confidence will improve, and you will further protect yourself from unwanted emotions.

The key to Building Mastery is that the activity needs to be challenging enough to feel like an accomplishment, but not so challenging that you set yourself up for failure, burnout, and shame. If you pick up a guitar for the very first time, you should aim to learn how to play a chord or two—not how to play your favorite song. Over time, of course, you will need to increase the level of difficulty to continue Building Mastery and feeling that sense of achievement.

One final note: People often avoid taking steps to Accumulate Positive Emotions and Build Mastery. Some people doubt that they will actually experience positive emotions by engaging in the activity; others are trying to avoid unpleasant emotions that might come up in the process; and some simply have trouble doing things when they don't feel motivated, even if they know logically that it will help. If you find yourself having the urge to procrastinate or avoid implementing these skills, be sure to try to access Wise Mind, and consider the pros and cons of avoiding. This is also a situation where your Opposite Action skills from Week 4 can really come in handy!

PLEASE Skills: Additional Strategies to Reduce Vulnerability to Unwanted Emotions

In addition to Accumulating Positive Emotions and Building Mastery, we can also increase our emotional resilience by taking care of our physical well-being. When we are physically not at our best, this can impact us emotionally too. For example, many people feel more anxious and irritable when they have not slept enough than when they are well rested. In DBT, we use the acronym PLEASE to highlight five aspects of your physical well-being to take care of in order to protect yourself from Emotion Mind:

+ treat **PhysicaL** illness
+ balance **E**ating
+ avoid mood-**A**ltering substances
+ balance **S**leep
+ get **E**xercise

Of course, addressing all of these is the most effective approach. That said, we find that simply being mindful of them can be helpful too. For example, just recognizing that your mood has been impacted by not getting enough sleep (or skipping a meal and getting "hangry") can make it easier to tolerate your increased anxiety and irritability, even if it's still unpleasant.

EXERCISE: *Identify Opportunities to Accumulate Positive Emotions in the Short Term*

To be thoughtful and effective in Accumulating Positive Emotions in the Short Term, the first step is to identify activities that bring up pleasant emotions for you. The goal in this exercise is to come up with a variety of options that you can begin to build into your life.

INSTRUCTIONS

1. List as many activities as you can think of that bring up positive emotions for you. Aim for a minimum of five (but don't stop there if you can come up with more!). While there is no right or wrong amount, it can be helpful to have a variety of options. If you need additional space, continue on another piece of paper.

2. You might find it helpful to think of activities that evoke different types of positive emotions—for example, joy, pleasure, relief, amusement, happiness, excitement, pride, love, or contentment.

3. Include activities that you know you enjoy or that at the very least you think there is a reasonable chance you would enjoy. Keep in mind that these do not need to create intense positive feelings (though that is acceptable too!); even mildly enjoyable activities count.

4. You can also search for "pleasant activities list," "pleasant events schedule," "self-care activities," or similar search terms on the internet to find ideas and examples.

continued

IDEAS FOR ACCUMULATING POSITIVE EMOTIONS IN THE SHORT TERM

1. ....
2. ....
3. ....
4. ....
5. ....
6. ....
7. ....
8. ....
9. ....
10. ....
11. ....
12. ....
13. ....
14. ....
15. ....

For some people, it can be difficult to come up with ideas for enjoyable or pleasant activities. It might be hard to find time in your busy schedule; finances might be a challenge; or you may simply be unable to think of options that you actually expect to enjoy. If this is the case for you, this is a great opportunity to put the Problem Solving skills that you learned in Week 5 to work!

EXERCISE: *Identify Your Values and Goals*

In this exercise, you will begin the process of Accumulating Positive Emotions in the Long Term by identifying some of your values and setting specific goals based on these values. This will allow you to take steps more mindfully toward living life in a way that feels personally meaningful, valuable, and fulfilling.

INSTRUCTIONS

1. In the first section on the next page, identify values that are important to you. Keep in mind that values are guiding principles rather than specific goals— for example, "be productive and hard working in my job" is a value, whereas "get a promotion at work" is a goal.

2. Many people find it challenging to identify their values. You might find it helpful to think of different life domains (e.g., work, education, leisure, relationships, physical/emotional/spiritual well-being) and the values you have for each. You can also search for "values inventory" or "values list" on the internet to find examples of common values.

3. From the list of values you have identified, select two or three that are high-priority values to you *right now*. Note that your values and priorities may change over time. For example, although you may always value being a supportive friend, it may be an even higher priority if you know a close friend is going through a difficult time.

4. Next, for each of your current high-priority values, identify goals related to that value. Remember that goals should be specific enough that you can clearly determine whether they have been achieved. Additionally, it is important to choose goals that are realistic in order to set yourself up for success.

continued

As you complete this exercise, you may find yourself questioning if something is truly a value for *you,* or if it's something you think you *should* value even though it isn't actually very important to you personally. Many of us experience this because we have been raised in families or communities that emphasize certain values that we don't actually share. It can be difficult to accept when your values differ from those of people or groups you care about. To get the most meaning and fulfillment from life, though, it is important to consider your personal values. For this exercise, use your Wise Mind to select values that are important to *you.*

VALUES OF MINE INCLUDE:

HIGH-PRIORITY VALUES RIGHT NOW	GOALS RELATED TO THIS VALUE

EXERCISE: *Take Steps Toward Your Goals*

In this exercise, you will move toward Accumulating Positive Emotions in the Long Term by choosing one value to focus on now and one goal related to this value. You will then determine the steps necessary to work toward this goal. This focused approach will decrease the likelihood that you get distracted, overwhelmed, or feel stuck.

INSTRUCTIONS

1. Choose *one* high-priority value you identified in the previous exercise, and select *one* goal related to that value that you would like to work on now. In deciding which goal to begin with, use your Wise Mind and consider how realistic each goal is as well as how important each one is to you.

2. Break down your goal into small, manageable steps. What is the very first step you would need to take toward this goal? What would come next? For example, if your goal is to find a romantic partner, the first step might be to download a dating app.

3. Take the first step!

Often we get stuck in our pursuit of a goal because the task feels too daunting, like there is a mountain in front of us to climb. The thing to keep in mind is that if you reach any step that feels too big, you can always break that down into smaller steps, too. For example, if the goal of downloading a dating app stops you in your tracks, you can break that down into smaller steps and begin by deciding which app to download. If you find yourself stuck on that decision, you can break that down into smaller steps and start by asking a friend about their experience with dating apps, or google the pros and cons of different apps.

TAKING STEPS TOWARD MY GOAL WORKSHEET

GOAL I WANT TO WORK ON NOW: _____

_____

STEPS TOWARD MY GOAL

1. _____

2. _____

3. _____

4. _____

5. _____

6. _____

7. _____

8. _____

9. _____

10. _____

EXERCISE: *Identify Opportunities to Build Mastery*

Building Mastery effectively often requires mindfully identifying and planning activities that generate feelings of capability and accomplishment. In this exercise, you will take a proactive approach to identifying and pursuing opportunities to Build Mastery.

INSTRUCTIONS

1. On the following page, list as many activities as you can think of that create feelings of competence, capability, accomplishment, pride, or self-confidence. What kinds of activities evoke these emotions for you? Are there things you already do, or that you have done in the past, that bring up these feelings? What about new ideas? Consider things you do at work or school, in your family or home life, "adulting" tasks, and personal hobbies and interests.

2. Remember that the key is for the activity to be at least a little bit challenging, without it being so difficult that you are unlikely to succeed. If you want to get better at cooking, for example, you might start with learning how to fry an egg rather than trying to make egg soufflé. Look at the ideas you have generated and, if necessary, edit what you have written to specify what would be in that "challenging but achievable" sweet spot for each.

3. You can also search "how to build mastery," "ideas for building mastery," or similar terms on the internet for ideas and examples.

continued

IDEAS FOR BUILDING MASTERY

_____

_____

_____

_____

_____

_____

_____

_____

_____

Many of us only experience feelings of mastery in one or two domains, but this can start to feel stale over time; you may find that you get a different kind of satisfaction from overcoming challenges in new or different contexts! For example, someone whose job is more analytical and intellectual might experience a different kind of mastery from doing something hands-on, like painting a room or learning to play a musical instrument; someone whose mastery comes from active pursuits like sports might enjoy learning a new language or playing chess. If you notice that the activities you listed all fall into the same one or two categories, consider whether you might find it valuable to try something new.

EXERCISE: *Schedule for Accumulating Positive Emotions and Building Mastery*

When Accumulating Positive Emotions and Building Mastery, it is important not to rely on activities that "fall into your lap" or are initiated by others, as this leaves too much to chance. In this exercise, you will plan and schedule activities that have the potential to be emotionally rewarding in order to increase the likelihood you actually experience more positive emotions.

INSTRUCTIONS

1. Look at the table on page 107. In the column under "Planned Activities," identify activities and action steps that you can take each day over the next five days. There is no need to reinvent the wheel here—use the lists you already came up with in the previous exercises! It may be helpful to schedule a specific time of day to increase the likelihood that you follow through with the plan. If you want to create a 7-day schedule, photocopy page 107 or download and print an extra copy of it (using the QR code on page 208) before filling it out.

2. While we certainly encourage you to try to engage in activities from all three categories every day, we realize that this isn't always realistic. As they say, "Don't let perfect be the enemy of good!" Plan and schedule an activity or step from at least one category per day, and use your Wise Mind to strike a balance between pushing yourself to work hard while also knowing the limits of what you can realistically accomplish.

3. Be sure to incorporate at least a few different activities or pleasant events rather than just repeating the same one every day. While you can certainly use the same activity more than once, having a variety of positive experiences and emotions can enhance the benefit you get from this process.

continued

4. Over the course of the week, fill out the "Notes" column to record comments to yourself about what the experience was like and any challenges you faced (e.g., "It was hard to enjoy because I was ruminating," "Way too hard—I need to try it again at a lower level of difficulty," or "I feel so proud of myself for finishing that!").

You know what they say about "the best-laid plans." Adding so many new events to your schedule can be a big change, and it can be easy to forget what you intended to do. Consider if it would be helpful to incorporate these activities into your daily calendar, set reminders on your phone, or put a copy of this worksheet somewhere you will see it to ensure you remember your action plan. If you find yourself tempted to avoid following through on these plans, remember to use Opposite Action and avoid that avoidance at all costs! Lastly, use your notes from the last column when you plan future pleasant events or mastery activities; they can help guide you toward the activities that were most valuable, or highlight what you might need to troubleshoot next time around.

My Schedule for Accumulating Positive Emotions and Building Mastery

DATE	PLANNED ACTIVITIES	NOTES
	Pleasant events: Steps toward goals: Mastery activities:	
	Pleasant events: Steps toward goals: Mastery activities:	
	Pleasant events: Steps toward goals: Mastery activities:	
	Pleasant events: Steps toward goals: Mastery activities:	
	Pleasant events: Steps toward goals: Mastery activities:	

DISTRESS TOLERANCE

Shutting down in depression. "Seeing red" in anger. Panicking in fear. Falling apart. These are all ways we might describe experiences of feeling totally overwhelmed by our emotions. In these situations, we can't think clearly and can't use complex skills like Checking the Facts or Problem Solving. If you ever feel this way, you've reached what DBT calls the "skills breakdown point." At this point, it's really difficult to access Wise Mind.

Luckily, DBT has skills for these exact moments. The "crisis survival skills" help us tolerate really painful situations without relying on impulsive behaviors that make things worse by hurting ourselves, hurting others, or causing ourselves other negative consequences. These skills, along with "reality acceptance" skills, make up the Distress Tolerance skills, and offer us freedom from this type of suffering. When we feel confident in our coping abilities, we feel a greater sense of control and peace, knowing that we can make it through whatever the world throws at us, even though it may still be painful. In the next three weeks, we'll cover skills that will help you cope more effectively with painful emotions, so that you can meet your life head-on.

Prepare for Stormy Weather

WEEK 7

Even if we wish it weren't the case, pain is a fact of life. Inevitably, we all face disappointments, obstacles, and stressors, and we can get into a lot of trouble if we don't know how to endure emotional pain without falling apart. This week, we'll provide you with a ton of skills to use during distress and offer some guidance about how to set yourself up for coping skills success.

What Is Distress Tolerance?

As the name suggests, Distress Tolerance skills help us *tolerate* distress. They help us experience our emotions without becoming overwhelmed or out of control. Distress Tolerance is particularly useful when we're in a crisis: a stressful, short-term situation with potentially negative consequences. Perhaps you get fired from your job or your significant other breaks up with you. In these crises, you might feel better in the short term if you act impulsively (e.g., yell obscenities at your boss) or avoid (e.g., cancel plans with friends because you don't want to talk about your ex), but you're likely to cause yourself more problems in the long run. For example, you might not get a recommendation for your next job or hurt your friends' feelings.

The DBT "crisis survival skills" are designed to help you cope with intense distress without making things worse. They can even help you feel better (though that isn't the goal of Distress Tolerance). But, these skills won't help if you don't use them! It helps to plan. In the same way it helps to physically prepare for major bad weather, it's essential to do the same for emotional storms. Consider this week's chapter your guide to "emotional emergency" preparation.

First Step in a Crisis: STOP

When in crisis, it's normal to have intense urges *to do something* to change the situation. These initial urges are often not the most helpful. The STOP skill helps you to stop yourself from reacting impulsively and to follow Wise Mind. You STOP in a crisis by following four steps:

+ **S**TOP

+ **T**AKE A STEP BACK

+ **O**BSERVE

+ **P**ROCEED MINDFULLY

In our experience, the easiest way to STOP (and act skillfully during a crisis) is to use an Emotion Regulation skill that we haven't introduced yet: Cope Ahead. The Cope Ahead skill involves identifying a potentially difficult situation, planning how to cope with it, and then *imagining* yourself using that plan to cope effectively. Research supports the idea that we can learn new skills by practicing them in our imagination, possibly because the same parts of the brain get activated whether we do a thing or *think* about doing that thing. In this week's exercises, we'll teach you how to actually do each of STOP's four steps, and you'll get practice Coping Ahead for crises.

The Power of Planning Ahead

Let's say you successfully complete the first step in your coping plan during your next crisis: you effectively STOP and don't engage in impulsive behaviors. Then what? You need options for coping with your distress! Luckily, DBT offers numerous strategies for just this purpose, captured by three sets of skills: distraction, self-soothing, and improving the moment.

DISTRACTION

Distraction involves purposefully bringing your attention away from the painful event that is prompting your emotions, and shifting it to something else more positive or neutral. Distraction can help you pass the time when your distressing problems can't be solved right now.

DBT offers several strategies for how to distract, following the acronym ACCEPTS:

- **A**CTIVITIES: watch TV, read a book, clean, scroll social media, go on a walk, or do anything that takes your full attention.

- **C**ONTRIBUTING: focus on other people rather than your problems. Volunteer, find things in your house to donate, do a favor for someone, or send a nice message to a friend.

- **C**OMPARISONS: compare yourself to others who are less fortunate to think about your current problem in a different light; think about times you felt or coped worse than now; watch reality TV.

+ **E**MOTIONS: do something to evoke different emotions than the one you're feeling. Watch a horror film when you're sad, listen to comedy when you're angry, or read a romance novel when you're anxious.

+ **P**USHING AWAY: push away thoughts or feelings. Imagine putting the problem on a shelf, on the backburner, or behind a wall. Deny the situation, temporarily.

+ **T**HOUGHTS: fill your mind with other thoughts to interrupt worry or rumination. Sing a song, do math in your head, or name colors or count objects around you.

+ **S**ENSATIONS: ground yourself with physical sensations. Take a hot or cold shower; chew on or hold ice; squeeze a stress ball; eat hot sauce, ginger chews, or sour candy.

SELF-SOOTHING

Our next set of crisis survival strategies is self-soothing: purposefully being soothing, nurturing, and physically kind to yourself when you're distressed. These strategies are unique to every person. To identify your self-soothing skills, consider what makes you feel pleasure, relaxed, happy, or soothed in each of your five senses. Here are some examples:

+ SIGHT: look at real or photographed nature, art, animals, flowers, or architecture; watch a candle burn; look at old photos of loved ones.

+ SMELL: burn a scented candle or incense; go into nature or open your window; bake cookies, boil herbs, or brew aromatic coffee/tea.

+ HEARING: go into nature or listen to recorded nature sounds; listen to your favorite music; listen to ASMR videos.

+ TASTE: treat yourself to comfort food; eat a favorite food; drink a favorite (nonalcoholic) drink; suck on candy.

+ TOUCH: get a massage; pet an animal; wear soft clothing; wrap yourself in a weighted or fluffy blanket; take a warm bath/shower.

IMPROVE THE MOMENT

Our final set of crisis survival skills includes ways you may be able to *improve* the moment and make it more positive. IMPROVE can be particularly handy when your current distress is from a situation that is longer lasting. Here are some ideas on how you can IMPROVE the moment when you're in a crisis:

+ **I**MAGERY: imagine your "safe space," picture yourself acting skillfully, reminisce on past positive memories, or fantasize about anything to escape a painful present moment temporarily.

+ **M**EANING: "find a silver lining" or "make lemonade out of lemons" by trying to find meaning or positive aspects in your situation. (Note: this does not mean simply saying "this is for the best" or "everything happens for a reason" if you don't believe that!) Read about other people coping with life's pain.

+ **P**RAYER: even if you're not religious, connecting with "something larger" can be helpful in painful times. Besides prayer or other spiritual practices, you could meditate, spend time with your community, or spend time in nature.

+ **R**ELAXING ACTIONS: do anything that relaxes you and slows you down. Massage yourself, breathe deeply, take a bath, drink something warm, light a candle, stretch or gently move your body.

+ **O**NE THING IN THE MOMENT: focus your entire attention on just this one moment to decrease worrying about the future or thinking about everything that has gone wrong in the past.

+ **V**ACATION: even if you can't literally go on vacation, give yourself a break. Turn your phone off, spend an afternoon in a park or at a beach, or get into bed for an hour. Take a brief vacation from life (in any way that won't cause you trouble!).

+ **E**NCOURAGEMENT AND RETHINKING THE SITUATION: rather than criticize yourself, talk to yourself the way you would talk to a loved one. Cheerlead yourself. Say things like, "I'll get through this," "I'm doing the best I can," or "This isn't forever."

Distraction, Self-Soothing, and IMPROVE provide various ideas for how to survive emotional distress without making things worse. The important thing here is that you eventually return to addressing the problem that caused the crisis in the first place, once you are no longer in Emotion Mind. While the crisis survival strategies can be helpful on a temporary basis, overusing them and avoiding distress entirely is likely to lead to crisis after crisis, because these strategies don't address the actual problems causing your distress. Instead, think of these skills as helpful ways to get the break that everyone needs at times.

One final distress tolerance skill that can be useful in these scenarios is Pros and Cons. When we're in Wise Mind, before a crisis, we can make a list of the pros and cons of using Distress Tolerance skills versus acting on impulsive urges during crises. Then, when we're in crisis, we can review that list to help ourselves access Wise Mind. You'll get to learn more about this skill and practice it in the upcoming exercises.

Think of these skills as essential supplies for your "emotional emergency" preparation. You can prepare for a crisis before it happens by stabilizing your mood (through the skills you learned last week), as well as creating a coping plan and assembling a "distress tolerance kit." This week's exercises will help you do just that.

EXERCISE: *Create a Distress Tolerance Kit*

When we're really distressed, we're often not thinking clearly, and it can be hard to remember new coping skills. Set yourself up for success by creating a Distress Tolerance kit that will be ready and waiting for you to use the next time you're in crisis.

INSTRUCTIONS

1. Consider all of the strategies from ACCEPTS, self-soothing, and IMPROVE. Think about which could help you tolerate your distress and get through a crisis without doing things that could make it worse. Choose skills that you've used successfully before, and new ones you're willing to try.

2. Designate a specific space and/or use a special container (e.g., a basket, toiletry bag, or decorated box) to act as your kit.

3. Fill the kit with the actual physical objects you might use to self-soothe (e.g., candy and photography book), distract (e.g., fidget spinners and a list of acts of kindness you could do), and IMPROVE the moment (e.g., a book of Rumi poetry and note of encouragement). For skills that can't be physically stored in your kit, write a note to remind yourself (e.g., "go grab ice" or "call Marcia").

You can make kits for anywhere—while traveling, at work or school, at dinner parties, wherever! We recommend making your first Distress Tolerance kit a "general" one for your home. Some of our clients have created "digital kits" for when they only have access to their phones. You can keep an app folder or note with a list of skills, mantras, YouTube links, playlists, or photos. Wherever your kit is, know it is always a work in progress. Throughout this week, we recommend you experiment and try new skills! Our clients have often been surprised by a "weird" or "corny" crisis survival skill working for them.

EXERCISE: *Pros and Cons*

The crisis survival skill of Pros and Cons can help you resist "problem behaviors" by bringing your attention to *all* the consequences that would come from engaging in them. Although you can use this skill in a moment of a crisis, it's *much* more effective to complete Pros and Cons beforehand when it's easier to access Wise Mind. We recommend you complete the exercise now for the impulsive behaviors you usually struggle with during crises.

INSTRUCTIONS

1. On page 119, name the problem behavior that your distress prompts for you during a crisis. For example: using substances, sending an angry text message, or avoiding doing work. (Note: if you have multiple problem behaviors, you should complete a separate Pros and Cons for each behavior.)

2. In the grid, identify the pros of acting on your crisis urge (i.e., engaging in your problem behavior). What positive consequences happen (both short term and long term) when you engage in this behavior—for example, immediate relief, feel validated, let my emotion out, receive support?

3. Next, identify the cons of acting on your crisis urge. What negative consequences happen when you engage in this behavior—for example, guilt/shame, hurt someone else, negative physical consequences, damage relationships, create new problems?

4. Identify the pros of resisting the crisis urge or using skills. What positive consequences happen when you resist the urges for this behavior, or use skills—for example, pride, improve relationships, keep commitments, receive support, personal growth?

continued

5. Next, identify the cons of resisting the crisis urge or using skills. What negative consequences happen when you resist the urges for this behavior—for example, takes effort, distress may last longer, confusion, discomfort, anxiety/fear?

6. Review all the pros and cons you identified. Make sure you've included both short-term and long-term consequences wherever relevant.

7. Circle or mark the consequences that are most important to you. For example, perhaps you know that during a crisis you will really want immediate relief from physical discomfort (i.e., a pro of acting on crisis urges), and you are really focused on improving your relationships right now (i.e., a pro of resisting crisis urges) and not breaking commitments (i.e., a con of acting on crisis urges).

Pros and Cons *usually* end up showing two things. First, it makes sense that you want to engage in impulsive behaviors—they work, at least in the sense that they often help you feel better in the short term! Second, your impulsive behaviors usually have more negative consequences than acting skillfully, especially in the long term. Reading your Pros and Cons grid repeatedly for a few days (or weeks) will make it more likely that you remember them when in crisis.

You can also review your grid when you're in Emotion Mind. Put the grid in your distress tolerance kit, keep a photo of it on your phone, or post it somewhere near where you commonly have crisis urges (e.g., on your fridge, in your bathroom, or by your bed). For some people, it's more useful to write out the 2–3 primary Pros and Cons and focus on those rather than the full grid. When having crisis urges, using Pros and Cons can help you access Wise Mind and validate yourself while still saying "no!"

PROBLEM BEHAVIOR/CRISIS URGE

_____

_____

	PROS	CONS
Acting on this urge		
Resisting this urge		

EXERCISE: *Coping Ahead for How to STOP in Crisis*

While you can Cope Ahead for acting effectively in any type of difficult situation, we're going to focus here on how you could use STOP and other crisis survival skills when you're very distressed. The most effective coping skills are likely to be at least a little different in different situations, so it will be useful to complete separate Cope Ahead plans for distinct types of crises, problem behaviors, or emotions.

INSTRUCTIONS

1. In the worksheet on page 123, describe the crisis, crisis urge, or emotion for which you want to Cope Ahead. Although you can't predict the future perfectly, use previous experiences to describe the anticipated situation. Most importantly, what would you be feeling? At the very least, identify your crisis urge and how you first experience that urge in your body or mind before emotions overwhelm you. There might be a *pressured* or agitated feeling. Get specific about what thoughts or physical sensations you feel as you're slipping into Emotion Mind.

2. Identify how you could **Stop**. How could you pause, freeze, and not react? You could clap your hands together, put a hand out in a "stop" gesture, say "stop!" aloud or in your head, or mentally picture a stop sign.

3. Identify how you could **Take a Step Back**. You could literally take a step back, away from a person or thing related to your problem behavior. You could sit down, turn around, close your eyes, or leave the room. You could close your computer or turn off your phone.

4. Identify how you could **Observe**. Use your mindfulness skills to check in with yourself and the situation. Take deep breaths and purposefully stretch or relax your body. Label your urges, feelings, or sensations and validate them ("I'm feeling really angry, and I really want to yell"). Describe the facts to yourself, or use the Check the Facts skill.

5. Identify how you could **Proceed Mindfully**. Practice Wise Mind, read your Pros and Cons, or consider what would be most effective based on the facts and your goals. Use your distress tolerance kit or ask someone for help. Like at a real stop sign, you don't STOP forever. You look both ways and move forward. Identify exactly what crisis survival skills you would use and in what order, followed by any other skills you would use to address the situation. (Be specific! Write "watch *Parks and Recreation* or *Schitt's Creek*" rather than "watch TV.")

6. Identify your ideal outcome. How would this crisis end if you act totally skillfully? How would you want to feel by the time you're finished with your skills? Describe in detail the outcome you desire.

7. Using the information from the above steps, imagine yourself following this Cope Ahead plan. Visualize it as if you are living it in real time, not just watching it as a spectator. As vividly as possible, picture yourself experiencing the initial crisis—your urges, emotions, and sensations—then visualize STOP-ing, acting skillfully, and reaching your desired outcome. If you struggle with mental imagery or visualization, write out a detailed script and reread it instead. You can also record yourself reading your script, and then listen to your recording. "Rehearse" your coping plan in your mind repeatedly.

continued

8. Finally, as you develop your Cope Ahead plan, notice if there is any-thing besides the scripting or rehearsing that you can do *right now* to help yourself succeed in your plan. Put your written-out plan in your distress tolerance kit. If you suspect you'll be in a certain place when you have problem behavior urges, you can put a picture of a stop sign there to remind yourself to STOP. Share your Cope Ahead plan with a friend, partner, roommate, or therapist who might be willing to sup-port you during a crisis. We also have included a DBT Skills Cheat Sheet on page 203—you can use it to craft a personalized list of the skills you find most helpful, and use it while developing your Proceed Mindfully plan!

If your crisis plan doesn't work the first time, that's okay. Coping with intense emotions is *hard*. Changing behavior is *hard*. One of the most common experiences during crises is feeling physical pressure to do something. These sensations are often what drive impulsivity, so deal-ing with them is likely going to be an important part of your crisis coping plan. While some skills from this week can help, next week we'll be giving you some skills specifically for the physical aspects of distress.

If you engage in your problem behavior this week despite Coping Ahead, don't get too down on yourself! Use some self-soothing skills and, when you feel ready, use your Problem Solving skills to reexamine the parts of your coping skills plan that didn't work. We have more skills in the upcoming chapters that might be helpful to incorporate into your plan as well!

CRISIS COPE AHEAD PLAN WORKSHEET

After completing this worksheet, remember to review your plan or imagine yourself implementing it.

1. What is the crisis/urge/emotion I want to Cope Ahead for? _____
   _____

2. What feelings, thoughts, or sensations will I observe before falling into
   Emotion Mind? _____
   _____
   _____
   _____

3. How I will STOP in that first moment: _____
   _____
   _____

4. How I will Take a Step Back: _____
   _____
   _____

5. How I will Observe: _____
   _____
   _____

6. How I will Proceed Mindfully: _____
   _____
   _____

7. How the crisis will end (ideally): _____
   _____
   _____

Use Your Body to Calm Down

WEEK 8

When overwhelmed by emotion, you might feel physically agitated and tense. Alternatively, your sense of being "overloaded" might translate into shutting down or spacing out. These experiences can be very uncomfortable and confusing, making you feel like you're out of control (even of your own mind and body). This week, we'll teach you how to understand these experiences, calm your body in distress, and ground yourself so that you can experience strong emotions without acting impulsively.

The Body's Stress Response

Last week, we introduced the idea of a "crisis" and how it's common in a crisis to feel a physiological *pressure* to do something. When feeling emotions intensely, you might feel some extra, uncomfortable energy. As we pointed out in Week 3, these physical sensations can generate helpful action urges. Often these physical sensations lead us to engage in unhealthy coping behaviors, though. What's going on here?

The nervous system is the primary communication and control system of the human body, reaching from the top of your head all the way down to your fingers and toes. Part of it (the **autonomic nervous system**, or ANS) keeps you alive without you needing to think about it, controlling your breathing, digestion, reflexes, and more. One part of the ANS, the **sympathetic nervous system**, controls your response to stress. When you're stressed, your sympathetic nervous system activates a lot of changes in your body: increased heart rate, faster breathing, and tense muscles, among others. These changes are what make up the "fight-flight-or-freeze" response, referring to the options that we have evolved for responding to danger.

Our bodies react in the same way to all kinds of stressors, even if they're not physically dangerous. If our stress is caused by a deadline at work or a difficult conversation with our partner, our bodies still prepare us for life-and-death reactions. When we don't use the energy of the stress response to fight or flee, often because neither of those options are actually useful, we are left with a lot of physical discomfort and may feel "overloaded," foggy, numb, or overtired. Whatever our stress response, our bodies are trying to help us. They just get a bit confused by the modern world.

Thankfully, the ANS has a second component: the **parasympathetic nervous system**. While the sympathetic nervous system leads to increased physiological arousal, the parasympathetic nervous system leads to the "rest-and-digest" response: reduced arousal, decreased heart rate, slower breathing, muscle relaxation, etc. In this recovery state, it's easier to think, connect with others, learn, play, and participate mindfully. The *really* cool thing is that there are ways we can deliberately activate the parasympathetic nervous system in order to deactivate the sympathetic nervous system. These are the final crisis survival skills we'll teach you: the TIP skills.

The TIP Skills

These skills are "biohacks" of a sort; they use the mind-body connection to reduce emotional distress by reducing physiological arousal. By directly impacting your body chemistry and the ANS, they are some of the most effective and fast-acting Distress Tolerance skills, once you get the hang of them. They're useful to throw into your STOP practices and crisis Cope Ahead plans.

TIP is an acronym and refers to a set of four skills:

✦ **T**EMPERATURE

✦ **I**NTENSE EXERCISE

✦ **P**ACED BREATHING

✦ **P**AIRED MUSCLE RELAXATION

TEMPERATURE

The first TIP skill—T, for Temperature—uses the **mammalian dive reflex** to calm us down by activating the parasympatheic nervous system. Most mammals, including humans, have a reflex that automatically lowers their heart rates when they are immersed in cold water. This reflex allows us air-breathing creatures to endure longer periods of time underwater. (Slower heart rates = less oxygen needed.) The Temperature skill activates the dive reflex by having you put your face in cold water. It's a really effective skill, though short-lived, so it's often useful to immediately follow the Temperature skill with other crisis survival skills. We'll give you more details on how to use the Temperature skill, and the other TIP skills, in this week's exercises.

INTENSE EXERCISE

The second TIP skill—I, for Intense Exercise—helps you calm down by getting out pent-up energy. Exercising on a regular basis helps reduce depression, anxiety, and anger. Even just *one* session of exercise can lessen negative emotions and generate positive emotions when we're in crisis! When you exercise intensely, you activate your sympathetic nervous system. You can purposefully activate the parasympathetic nervous system by consciously stretching or relaxing after exercise. This skill can act like a hard reset for your body when it's overcome by distress.

PACED BREATHING

With the third TIP skill—P, for Paced Breathing—we use slowed, measured breath to ground ourselves. When we're relaxed, we naturally breathe more slowly and deeply. When stressed or emotionally agitated, we breathe more quickly and shallowly. In Paced Breathing, we use something called diaphragmatic breathing to take deep breaths into our bellies. We also make our exhales particularly long as another biohack: normally, our heart beats faster while we breathe in, and it beats slower while we breathe out. By purposefully breathing the way we breathe when we're relaxed, we can activate the parasympathetic nervous system.

PAIRED MUSCLE RELAXATION

The final TIP skill—P, for Paired Muscle Relaxation (PMR)—is a strategy for using the mind-body connection to calm down by pairing deep exhales with muscle relaxation. You systematically go through your whole body, tensing muscles then mindfully releasing them. Similar to Intense Exercise, PMR is like a hard reset—your muscles will become more relaxed than they would if you tried relaxing without first tensing. You will further amplify this deeper relaxation by pairing the release of each muscle with a deep exhale, thinking "relax" in your mind, and focusing on how it feels to be relaxed.

Each of the four TIP skills can be useful to calm your body during crisis, reconnect with your Wise Mind in the present moment, and survive even the most difficult and physically uncomfortable emotional experiences.

EXERCISE: *Tip Your Temperature*

The Temperature skill can work *so* well at changing your physiological state that people with cardiac issues have to be careful with it. Consult your medical provider if you have any history of cardiovascular problems. While even splashing cold water on your face can be a really useful grounding exercise, there are a few specific steps to fully activate the dive reflex and get the most out of this skill.

INSTRUCTIONS

1. Gather your materials. You'll need a bowl (or a sink you can plug up) that is large enough for your face to fit into, ice, and a towel. No bowl/sink? Grab a flexible ice pack or bag of frozen vegetables and a paper towel.

2. Fill the bowl/sink with cold water and a big handful of ice cubes. You want the water to be cold, but not painfully so. If you're using an ice pack, wet the paper towel until it's thoroughly damp and wrap it around the pack.

3. Take a deep breath. With a bowl/sink, submerge just your face fully into the water. With an ice pack, hold the pack against your face, making sure it covers your eyes and nose/nostrils, and bend over. (This is key for activating the dive reflex!) Hold your breath for as long as you *comfortably* can.

4. After you remove your face from the water (or remove the ice pack from your face), take a few breaths as slowly as you can, and then repeat Step 3. Often 2–4 times is enough, but you can repeat as many times as you want. Add ice to the bowl if the water gets lukewarm.

When you're in Emotion Mind, you may not feel capable of getting all of the materials for this skill together. Help yourself by preparing them ahead of time in your distress tolerance kit (page 116).

EXERCISE: *Intense Exercise*

Stress leads to urges to fight or flee to safety. When we're emotionally aroused and then exercise, we're letting the body do what it wants to do—move! While any kind of movement can help, the skill of Intense Exercise works best when you bring your heart rate high enough. (Again, consult your medical provider before trying any new kind of exercise!)

INSTRUCTIONS

1. Choose a form of exercise that you are physically capable of doing, that you feel willing to do, and that will get your heart rate to moderate intensity. You can estimate your heart rate during exercise by talking out loud as if you were having a conversation with someone. If you're able to talk normally, your heart rate is too low. If you're only able to get a word or few out at a time, your heart rate is too high. At moderate intensity, you'll be able to speak about one sentence before needing to catch your breath.

2. Exercise! Whether you're using exercise as a TIP skill to calm down immediately, or you're trying to improve your overall mood by exercising regularly, it's most effective to exercise for 20–30 minutes at a time.

3. Stretch and relax when you're done exercising to purposefully lower your heart rate.

While you'll get the biggest bang for your buck by exercising at moderate intensity for at least 20 minutes, we know that's not always possible. Even one minute of Intense Exercise can be useful to calm down when you're past your skills breakdown point, because it's a great way to distract from your thoughts. Some of our and our clients' favorite quick exercises include jumping jacks, push-ups, squats, or yoga flows.

EXERCISE: *Paced Breathing*

There are three main features of Paced Breathing: inhaling through your nose, breathing into your belly, and elongating your exhales. When you're distressed, changing your breathing in any of these ways will be helpful for calming you down. Using all three will help the most.

INSTRUCTIONS

1. Sit in a comfortable, upright position with your legs uncrossed. Have a clock or timer in front of you that you can watch while breathing to count the seconds of your inhales and exhales.

2. If you've never practiced diaphragmatic breathing or "belly breathing" before, follow the instructions in this step before going into Paced Breathing. Lightly place your hands on your stomach, below your ribs, around your belly button. See if you can breathe deeply *into your belly* so that you feel your hands moving along with your inhales and exhales. Your shoulders should not move up and down. You also should not breathe so deeply that you feel tension or pain in your chest. If you're feeling confused, googling "how to belly breathe" should bring up some additional resources.

3. Before you begin Paced Breathing, choose a pattern of breathing in which your exhale is longer than your inhale. For example, one pattern is inhaling for 4 seconds and exhaling for 6; with 10 seconds for each whole breath, this timing allows for 6 even breaths in one minute. Some people also like to hold their breath between inhaling and exhaling, between exhaling and inhaling, or both. A common pattern is called "4-7-8 breath"—you inhale for 4 seconds, hold for 7, and exhale for 8. Choose any pattern you like, as long as the exhale is longer than the inhale.

4. To practice Paced Breathing, get in a comfortable position and place your hands softly on your lap or on your belly. When you're ready, begin diaphragmatic breathing, inhaling through your nose and exhaling through your mouth, according to the timing pattern you chose in Step 3. When exhaling, lightly purse your lips. You can think about inhaling like you're smelling a birthday cake and exhaling like you're blowing out the candles.

5. Continue Paced Breathing until you feel more grounded. It may very well take more than 10 minutes to feel less tense or agitated.

Paced Breathing is a versatile skill. Although it may not work as quickly as the other TIP skills, you can use it anywhere, anytime, around anyone, relatively invisibly. It's also a very effective skill to use routinely, even when you're not in crisis, to ground yourself, activate the parasympathetic nervous system, and reduce your vulnerability to unwanted emotions. If you'd like more structured guidance while breathing, you can find lots of videos by searching "paced breathing," "478 breathing," or "box breathing" on YouTube.

EXERCISE: *Paired Muscle Relaxation*

In PMR, we allow our bodies to do what they want to do when stressed—tense up, but then relax. When you are struggling with injury or illness and can't exercise in order to work through your stress response, PMR is a handy option. In the next steps, you will systematically tighten and loosen the various muscles in your body, starting at your toes and going up to your head.

INSTRUCTIONS

1. The first time you practice PMR, it's useful to give yourself enough time to go slowly through your whole body and get the hang of it. Lie down or sit in a comfortable position, with legs and arms uncrossed and with your head resting against something. Take a few deep belly breaths.

2. Starting at your feet, as you inhale or hold your breath, tighten your muscles (curl your toes and point them in toward each other to flex your ankles). Hold the position stiffly for at least four seconds—you should feel notable tension in the muscles of your feet, but you should *not* feel pain.

3. Quickly release all the tension in your feet and ankles, letting them fall totally limp like a rag doll. At the same time, exhale deeply, releasing your breath as you release your muscles, and say "relax" softly to yourself in your mind. Stay here for a few slow breaths, bringing your full attention to what it feels like for your feet muscles to be relaxed. You can repeat the word "relax" in your mind on the exhales while you do so.

4. Move up the body, repeating Steps 2 and 3, tightening then releasing/relaxing each muscle group in your body. Here is a potential order to follow:

+ feet, calves (point your toes down)

+ thighs (tense the fronts and backs of your upper legs)

+ butt (squeeze buttocks together)

+ stomach (suck or hold in abs)

+ back (arch your back, bringing shoulder blades toward each other and down)

+ upper arms (bend your arms at the elbow, squeeze your hands toward/against your shoulders)

+ lower arms and hands (clench your fists and pull them up toward your wrist)

+ shoulders (hunch up your shoulders toward your ears)

+ neck (push your head back against the ground/chair)

+ mouth (clench your jaw and push your tongue against the roof of your mouth)

+ face (pucker your lips, scrunch your nose, shut your eyes, and furrow your brow)

continued

5. After finishing all muscle groups, scan up and down your body. If you notice tension has reappeared anywhere, relax that muscle—you can briefly tighten and release again, if needed. Observe how your body feels loose and relaxed. Take a few deep breaths. Sit or stand up slowly when you are finished.

The more you practice PMR, the easier it will be for you to consciously relax your body. As you gain experience, you will be able to relax/ release multiple muscle groups at a time rather than one by one. If you practice daily, you may eventually be able to relax your entire body all at once, perhaps even just by saying "relax" to yourself in your mind. Regular practice also will improve your *interoception*, your awareness of your internal body. This will allow you to notice your stress sooner by becoming more mindful of tension in your body, which in turn will increase your ability to calm yourself *before* you reach a crisis point.

EXERCISE: *Tracking Your TIP Skills*

The TIP skills use the power of your body's nervous system to cope. This final exercise asks you to practice each of the TIP skills at least once this week, even if you don't experience any crisis, and provides a space for you to track all of your practices.

INSTRUCTIONS

1. This week, practice the Temperature, Intense Exercise, Paced Breathing, and Paired Muscle Relaxation skills. Practice each skill at least once, and practice as much as you can. Use the worksheet on the next page to track your practices.

2. Before each practice, circle the TIP skill you're practicing and rate how emotionally aroused or activated you feel on a scale of 1 through 10.

3. Practice your chosen TIP skill. After you've completed the skill, rate how aroused or activated you feel now on a scale of 1 through 10.

4. Jot down notes about your experience, including any tips for improving the skill's efficacy for next time.

All of the TIP skills are immensely powerful tools. While this chapter introduced TIP as skills to use when you're in crisis or acutely distressed, practicing these skills regularly can also reduce your overall emotional vulnerability by helping you feel calmer and less burned out. They help our bodies recover from stress and intense emotions, even when we are not in crisis. Additionally, the more you practice them in general, the easier it will be for you to use them when a crisis *does* occur.

continued

Exercise: Tracking Your TIP Skills *continued*

DATE	TIP SKILL(S) USED (circle)	AROUSAL BEFORE/AFTER (0-10)	NOTES (How did I practice, how did the skill help, what would I do differently next time, etc.)
	T I P P	/	
	T I P P	/	
	T I P P	/	
	T I P P	/	
	T I P P	/	
	T I P P	/	

Practice
Radical
Acceptance

WEEK 9

Sometimes life is not what we hoped for. While we can problem solve many things that cause us pain, we all inevitably encounter problems that can't be solved and issues that we have little-to-no control over. Learning how to cope with these situations is vital to reducing suffering. This week, we'll cover some final Distress Tolerance skills for increasing your sense of freedom and serenity when faced with painful realities.

What Is Radical Acceptance?

As we described in the introduction to this book, DBT was developed as a balance between change and acceptance. Acceptance involves being fully present (i.e., practicing mindfulness) and being open to reality exactly as it is rather than how we think it should be or wish it would be. Right away, we want to be clear about two things: acceptance does not mean approval, and it does not mean giving up. It may be easier to think about acceptance as *acknowledgment* of the facts of your life, even when you don't like the facts. Acceptance means being completely willing to work within a reality in which these painful facts exist.

Nonacceptance, in contrast, takes many forms: resenting reality; refusing to take effective steps within the context of your life; or feeling fierce indignation, despair, or shame about the facts of your life. In nonacceptance, you might notice judgmental, "should," or "why me" thoughts such as: "It's all my fault. I shouldn't be upset. It's all his fault. It shouldn't be this way. I should be able to fix this. Why does this always happen to me? This isn't fair." Nonacceptance leaves you feeling stuck in life, because denying or avoiding painful facts doesn't make them go away.

Instead, acknowledging painful facts allows you to feel and express your emotions fully, offering you the opportunity to get support from others and ultimately experience the peace that often follows when we grieve our reality. In other words, acceptance of what is painful in your life won't get rid of your pain, but it can reduce the suffering that is added on to your pain when you reject your reality. Additionally, at times acceptance can actually lead to decreased pain, because you can effectively solve problems only after you fully acknowledge them.

Radical Acceptance entails accepting reality with your full body, mind, and soul. It requires acting opposite *all the way* by doing what is needed to live a life that you still experience as meaningful and fulfilling, even when there is pain. Let's say you struggle with infertility when all you've wanted is to be a parent. Radically accepting infertility does not mean pretending that you never wanted children anyway, and it doesn't mean giving up on life now that you can't have your own biological children. It doesn't even necessarily mean giving up on becoming pregnant. Rather, Radical

Acceptance means allowing yourself to grieve, letting go of thinking about how unfair it is or whose fault it is, and trying to find meaning and pleasure in other ways. For example, you could choose to adopt, foster, volunteer with a children's organization, or pursue a life goal that would have been more difficult to pursue if you had children.

In Radical Acceptance you do not ignore pain and sadness, and you take steps to find fulfillment within the circumstances of the life you have (rather than the life you imagined). In meeting life head-on with Radical Acceptance, you can increase your sense of freedom by taking control of whatever you can when the world throws you curveballs (or when you feel like your life is one big curveball).

When to Radically Accept

Radical Acceptance is most useful, and arguably necessary, in a few types of situations. First, you must acknowledge your past and your present, especially when they're painful. You only have to accept the facts, not any interpretations or judgments you have about the facts. For example, you need to accept that you are aging, perhaps that you have gray hairs or wrinkles you did not have before, but you do not need to accept that now you're "ugly" or your skin is "gross."

Radical Acceptance of the past and present is extremely important (and particularly difficult) when you have experienced traumas or are currently facing major difficulties. The past is the past, and you cannot change it. Similarly, there are some features of reality you may have no direct power over, such as the way you're treated because of your gender or the color of your skin. We're *not* saying you need to accept that things are never going to change, or be "okay" with it. Rather, you need to radically accept the situation for what it is *right now*.

Notably, you do not need to accept most things about the future, primarily because they are all technically interpretations (since we can't predict the future). Accepting how your past and present reality may limit your future, however, can be helpful, as it supports realistic goal setting. If you're under a certain height, you're less likely to become an NBA player. If you have a history of stealing from or lying to your parents, it is more likely that they are going to have trouble trusting you. While accepting limitations on your future may cause sadness, it can increase your happiness in the long run because you're more likely to avoid failures when your goals are more attainable. Radical Acceptance of reasonable limitations on the future will also help you be appropriately prepared to spend the energy and effort required by difficult goals.

Finally, you need Radical Acceptance when you're in distress and can't change your situation right now, or when all your attempts at problem solving haven't yet worked, as in the infertility example on the previous pages. If something is painful and can't be changed (right now, or ever), relying on crisis survival skills is often ineffective because they just serve as a distraction from reality rather than helping you learn to live fully within reality. Radical Acceptance, instead, can help soothe your pain by offering space to feel your emotions and by shifting your focus back to building a Life Worth Living, even when life is hard or just really sucks.

How to Radically Accept

Acceptance can feel like an ambiguous and abstract concept. Luckily, there are a few concrete strategies you can use to practice reality acceptance, several of which involve accepting with the body. When we're not accepting, we are often experiencing some form of frustration or resentment of reality, and our bodies tense up. Muscles tighten, fists clench, and faces scowl or scrunch—much like they do when we're angry for any reason. Many of the body-based DBT skills you've learned previously may help with nonacceptance, including mindfulness of physical sensations, Paced Breathing, and relaxing actions. Two specific reality acceptance skills, **Half-Smiling** and **Willing Hands**, may be helpful as well. We'll teach you these and other skills more in-depth during this week's exercises.

To radically accept, you also must act opposite *all the way* to nonacceptance. In addition to relaxing your body, you must bring your thoughts and behaviors in line with acceptance. To practice Radical Acceptance in your thoughts, you can use self-talk. Explicitly remind yourself: "This is reality," "That happened," or "This is how things are right now." It may be helpful to consider the "causes" of reality; for example, reminding yourself of how you got to where you are, or how the world became what it became (if you know these things). The key is to do this completely nonjudgmentally, bringing your attention to the facts.

Alternatively, you can simply say to yourself: "It could be no other way" or "Things had to happen that way." Have self-compassion, avoid catastrophizing, and use Wise Mind self-encouragement. You can say to yourself: "I can figure this out," "I can survive this," or "I can build a joyful life."

To practice Radical Acceptance in your behaviors, you can act as if you have already radically accepted. Act opposite to willfulness. Willfulness is refusing to engage in reality as it is, denying the facts, or ignoring what is true or needed in the moment. **Willingness**, on the other hand, is participating in life fully, wisely, and effectively. To be willing and accepting, you can ask yourself: "If I were truly radically accepting reality, is there anything I would be doing differently in my life right now?" If so, find willingness, and do it. As with acting opposite to unwanted emotions, you will find that the more you act as if you radically accept something, the more you will come to actually accept it.

Radical Acceptance is extraordinarily hard. Sometimes acceptance lasts only moments. For the major losses or frustrations in your life, you'll need to repeatedly choose acceptance. In DBT we call this **Turning the Mind**, which requires you to notice when you're nonaccepting and then mindfully make a commitment to accept, over and over again. It's normal to experience intense fear, anger, or other overwhelming emotions when you are not accepting reality. Coping Ahead for these moments can be a useful tool.

When Radical Acceptance Feels Too Hard

No matter how effectively you Cope Ahead, you will still struggle at times with Radical Acceptance. When you struggle, first review your reality acceptance skills. Make sure you're using the strategies in this chapter fully. Next, check to see if you have any faulty beliefs getting in the way of acceptance; remind yourself that acceptance does not mean approval, acceptance does not mean giving up, and acceptance is required for change. Challenge any self-invalidating, judgmental, or hopeless thoughts you may have.

Next, cope fully with any strong emotions that are present. Check the Facts and use crisis survival skills as needed. Finally, when the above suggestions don't work and you feel totally stuck in willfulness or nonacceptance, ask yourself: "What's the threat?" Are you telling yourself that if you were to accept this, it would mean something unacceptable (about you, your future, or the world in general)? Are you scared you won't be able to cope with that catastrophe? If so, use Cope Ahead again! Figure out how you would use all the other DBT skills you've learned, even if the catastrophe happens, and remind yourself that you will be able to survive and thrive.

Note: All the exercises in this chapter may bring up intense emotions, because we are asking you to purposefully bring to mind some of the most painful events in your life. Consider keeping your Distress Tolerance kit nearby.

EXERCISE: *Identifying What You Need to Radically Accept*

The first step of Radical Acceptance is recognizing that you are not accepting reality. It's easy to get caught up in denial and avoidance, such that you don't even realize you're fighting reality. To be willing to accept reality, you must first notice the ways in which you're not. This exercise will help you practice this skill.

INSTRUCTIONS

1. On the next page, list out six things about your reality (e.g., situations, events, or facts) that you currently need to radically accept, putting each on its own line. Choose three things that are important or very difficult for you to accept, and three that are less painful or not as much of a "big deal." (Friendly reminder: acceptance does not mean approval.)

2. The "major" things you need to accept might evoke some stronger emotions, including grief or rage. Some examples include personal, familial, or cultural traumas; deaths of loved ones; failures or goals you did not achieve; or being unable to pursue a dream of yours that would require sacrifices that you're not able/willing to make right now. (Note: there is no right or wrong answer here, and what is a "major" thing is personal and subjective.)

3. The "minor" things you need to accept might feel like inconveniences or letdowns. Disappointment and irritation (at others, yourself, or the world) are common experiences. Some examples are your roommate's "annoying little habit"; obstacles outside of your control; feeling an emotion intensely; or not getting something you wanted. (Of course, some of these "minor" things may bring up intense emotions at times!)

continued

4. Now, double-check that there aren't any judgments, interpretations, or assumptions sneaking into your list. As needed, rewrite any items using the Nonjudgmentally skill you practiced during Week 1. For example, rather than "I'm broken," you might write, "I have trouble trusting others because of what I've been through." Or, rather than "I'm going to be alone forever," you might write, "My past five dates have been unpleasant," "I don't have as many friends as I want," or both (you may need to practice accepting each separately). Your nonjudgmental rewrite may be just as painful or difficult to radically accept. When you *accurately* accept what you need to accept, though (i.e., reality as it is), you will cope or problem solve more effectively, even as you feel painful emotions.

"MAJOR" THINGS I NEED TO RADICALLY ACCEPT

1. ....

2. ....

3. ....

"MINOR" THINGS I NEED TO RADICALLY ACCEPT

1. ....

2. ....

3. ....

Good news: if you've completed this exercise, you've already started the process of radically accepting. Well done practicing one of the hardest DBT skills! If you felt any emotions while completing this exercise and then practiced mindfulness of those emotions, even better. A huge part of Radical Acceptance is allowing yourself to feel sadness, disappointment, or grief that is understandable and justified; this is often what makes Radical Acceptance so tough. Use crisis survival skills (particularly self-soothing) whenever you need.

EXERCISE: *Half-Smiling and Willing Hands*

Half-Smiling and Willing Hands are ways to practice Radical Acceptance with your body by softening your facial expressions and hands. These strategies help you Act Opposite to the common action urges you likely experience when you're frustrated with reality. For your first practice of these skills, bring to mind something that is only somewhat irritating (rather than rage-inducing) so it's a bit easier.

INSTRUCTIONS

1. Sit in a comfortable position with closed fists in your lap, and bring to mind something or someone that you dislike or find frustrating. For example, you can think of one of the "minor" things you need to radically accept from the previous exercise, or a recent conflict you had with someone.

2. Imagine this person, remember the conflict, or think about the situation that has caused you suffering. Notice any tension that arises in your body, particularly in your face and your arms.

3. First, practice Half-Smiling. Relax all the muscles in your face—unfurrow your brow, let go of any tension in your cheeks, let your tongue drop from the roof of your mouth, and let your teeth drop slightly apart within your mouth. Then, ever so slightly, bring the corners of your lips up; this "half smile" should not feel tense and forced, and will likely not even be visible to anyone watching you.

4. Next, practice Willing Hands. Relax all the muscles in your upper body—drop your shoulders, let your arms hang loosely, gently open your palms upward, and relax your hands and fingers. (It's okay if your fingers naturally curl in this position.)

5. Continue to think about the thing that frustrates you, and notice how your body feels now in your new position. If you notice muscle tension return, intentionally soften your hands or facial muscles. Take deep belly breaths to further your relaxation.

EXERCISE: *Cope Ahead for Turning the Mind*

This exercise will help you plan ahead for how you might Turn the Mind when you're nonaccepting. Coping Ahead will increase the likelihood that you act willingly and practice Radical Acceptance. It will help you feel a greater sense of mastery over dealing with the unavoidable pains in your life.

INSTRUCTIONS

1. First, choose something that you anticipate finding difficult to accept. This might be something you repeatedly struggle with accepting, or it might be something you anticipate happening in the future.

2. Describe what you expect to be able to notice in a moment when you are not accepting. Will you have certain emotions, sensations, or judgmental thoughts? How does it look when you fight, deny, or avoid this reality?

3. Identify how you can Turn the Mind. How will you turn toward acceptance? You could say aloud "I will choose to radically accept this," or remind yourself of the pros and cons of accepting versus rejecting reality.

4. Identify how you would then practice Radical Acceptance. You could Nonjudgmentally Describe the facts that you need to accept, or practice Paced Breathing, relaxation techniques, Half-Smiling, or Willing Hands.

5. Finally, identify how you could practice Willingness and Participate fully in life. How could you avoid avoidance, solve problems related to the situation, or take steps toward your Life Worth Living? How could you allow yourself to feel your justified emotions? How could you Act Opposite to nonacceptance, and unjustified emotions associated with it?

RADICAL ACCEPTANCE COPE
AHEAD PLAN WORKSHEET

1. What is the thing I will need to radically accept? _____
_____

2. What feelings, thoughts, sensations, or behaviors will I observe in
   nonacceptance? _____
   _____
   _____
   _____
   _____

3. How will I Turn the Mind? _____
   _____
   _____
   _____
   _____

4. How will I practice Radical Acceptance? _____
   _____
   _____
   _____
   _____

5. What will I do to willingly, effectively, and wholeheartedly engage in reality?
   _____
   _____
   _____
   _____
   _____

EXERCISE: *A Week of Radical Acceptance*

The reality acceptance skills are considered part of Distress Tolerance because we use these skills to survive particularly painful moments. The more you practice them, the more your confidence in your ability to cope with even the hardest parts of your life will increase.

INSTRUCTIONS

1. Take time this week to practice Radical Acceptance using the skills and strategies we've introduced in this chapter (listed in the table on the next page). You can practice accepting the things you identified in the first exercise, or accepting new situations, events, or facts that come up during the week.

2. Be sure to use your crisis survival and Accumulating Positive Emotions skills, too. How can you self-soothe after acceptance practices? What pleasurable activities can you schedule?

3. Finally, we strongly recommend that you actively reward or care for yourself after practicing Radical Acceptance, since it can be draining and difficult.

As this week is dedicated to the reality acceptance skills, we encourage you to practice these as much as possible this week. That said, these skills are particularly challenging. We recommend that you keep using the following worksheet to track your practices over the next few weeks if you need to spread them out.

REALITY ACCEPTANCE SKILL	WHEN AND HOW I PRACTICED	HOW DID THIS SKILL HELP ME ACCEPT REALITY?	WHAT DID I LEARN FROM THIS PRACTICE?
Mindfulness of emotions			
Relaxation or breathing techniques			
Half-Smiling			
Willing Hands			
Reminded myself that reality is what it is			
Considered causes of reality			
Used self-encouragement			
Acted Opposite to nonacceptance			
Turned the Mind			
Did pros and cons of accepting vs. not			
Coped Ahead for acceptance			

INTERPERSONAL EFFECTIVENESS

Our relationships with other people are often what bring up the strongest emotions—and emotions also present significant challenges in our relationships, causing us to say or do things that our Wise Minds wish we wouldn't. The Interpersonal Effectiveness skills are all about how to communicate in ways that protect and enhance your relationships, address conflicts or issues when they arise, and get you more of what you want, all while leaving you feeling a greater sense of self-respect. These skills are crucial—after all, it's hard for just about anyone to feel satisfied in life without fulfilling, stable relationships.

Developing these skills will also create a positive feedback loop—the more effective you are interpersonally, the stronger your relationships will be. Healthier relationships will decrease your vulnerability to unwanted emotions and improve your self-esteem, which in turn will make it even easier to continue being interpersonally effective and strengthening your relationships. Ultimately, this will allow you to form fulfilling connections with people who respect your needs and limitations, support you, and help you build your larger Life Worth Living.

Approach Your Relationships Mindfully

WEEK 10

Relationships can feel like a minefield. We have all been there: hurt by something another person did but unsure how to handle it. "Do I say something here? I want to be honest about how I feel. Then again, if I'm honest, I might upset them or drive them away. But if I bite my tongue, nothing will change, and I'll just feel bad about myself. . . ." This week, we will introduce two sets of skills to help you begin to map out your path through the minefield and determine how to best balance competing desires.

What Do You Really Want?

Have you ever been in a situation in which you felt angry or hurt by someone, and after expressing your feelings, the person apologized—yet you still didn't feel satisfied? (Or perhaps you have been on the other side, saying sorry and then feeling confused when the other person continued as though you didn't apologize?) The problem is likely that getting an apology wasn't the primary thing you wanted! You might have wanted an explanation, validation, or a commitment from the other person to act differently in the future. This is one of the most common factors that interferes with communicating effectively: if you don't know what you want, it is much harder to get it! Therefore, the foundation of effective communication is clarifying your goals in the situation.

This is further complicated by the fact that in any interpersonal situation, we are actually juggling three different types of goals. In other words, there are three different areas that make up being interpersonally effective:

- ✦ OBJECTIVES EFFECTIVENESS refers to how to get what you want in the situation. Your Objective is generally the reason you are having the conversation in the first place. Some common examples include getting the other person to agree to something; saying no; obtaining an apology; or having your opinion heard.

- ✦ RELATIONSHIP EFFECTIVENESS refers to how to maintain or improve your relationship while trying to get what you want. It's normal for other people to have different priorities than you in a given situation, so Relationship Effectiveness is about how to protect the relationship even as you try to get your needs or desires met. This includes acting in a way that makes the other person feel as though you care about their feelings too—for example, focusing on listening to and understanding each other rather than on "winning" or proving that you're right.

- ✦ SELF-RESPECT EFFECTIVENESS refers to how to get through the interaction without undermining your self-respect—and (hopefully) even improving it. This includes behaving in the conversation in a way that leaves you feeling proud rather than ashamed—for example, if you tend to feel bad about yourself for yelling or crying, or for backing down rather than standing up for yourself. It also includes not agreeing to do something that compromises your values, as this also damages one's self-respect.

Keeping all these balls in the air at the same time isn't easy! We will introduce specific communication strategies for increasing Objectives Effectiveness, Relationship Effectiveness, and Self-Respect Effectiveness in the next two weeks. The starting point in any situation, however, is identifying your goals in each of these areas. This is a skill in its own right, and you'll have the opportunity to practice this in the first exercise this week.

But If You Can't Have Your Cake and Eat It Too . . .

Once you have identified your goals, the next step is to prioritize among them. Ideally, you will be able to achieve all three—and we recommend starting out any interaction trying to do just that! Unfortunately, sometimes it isn't possible to accomplish one without compromising on another. For example, if the only way to get someone to agree to a specific request is by not taking no for an answer, you might need to choose between getting that request met and not rocking the boat in the relationship.

Prioritizing in advance is particularly important because once you are already in the conversation, it is all too easy to act based on Emotion Mind or Reasonable Mind if you haven't yet identified your Wise Mind priorities. To continue with the previous example: if you tend to back down easily because you are generally afraid of angering or disappointing other people, you might automatically drop your request at the first sign of resistance. If you have determined that the objective is your Wise Mind priority, though, you will be more likely to continue asserting yourself—and therefore increase the likelihood that you actually get what you want.

Determining How Intensely to Communicate

In addition to Clarifying Priorities, a second skill that can set the stage for effective communication is determining how intensely to express what you want. While at times it's best to be gentle and prepared to take no for an answer, at other times it is necessary to be direct, firm, and even unrelenting. There are two components to this process: knowing how to express yourself at different levels of intensity, and considering the various factors that should inform your level of intensity in each situation.

One of the challenges in modulating intensity is that many people have a "default" level. Some tend to be softer and more deferential or even resist speaking up for themselves at all; others typically ask clearly or even bluntly for what they want; and some people live in the middle, rarely veering to either extreme.

This presents two problems. First and foremost, your default level of intensity may not be the right fit for every situation. For example, an emergency calls for communicating strongly what is needed: "You, call 911 right away!" rather than "Excuse me, if it's not too much trouble would you mind calling 911, please?" Secondly, if you always express yourself at the same level of intensity, other people may have trouble accurately reading when something is truly important to you. After all, if you sound the same whether you would prefer something or you desperately need it, how is the other person supposed to tell the difference and respond accordingly?

The options for level of intensity can be seen in the table on the next page. The left column applies to situations in which you would like to ask for something; the right column applies to situations in which you want to say no to another person's request. As you can see, level of intensity can range from not asking at all (or giving in) on one extreme to not taking no for an answer (or refusing to budge) on the other, with numerous points in between.

HOW TO ASK	INTENSITY LEVEL	HOW TO SAY NO
Don't ask at all	1	Anticipate the other person's request and do it before they even ask
Hint indirectly at what you want, and let it go easily if you don't get it	2	Say yes cheerfully, without complaining at all
Hint openly and clearly at what you want, and let it go easily if you don't get it	3	Say yes, but do so in a neutral manner (i.e., not cheerfully, but also not explicitly showing that you prefer not to)
Ask in a tentative way for what you want, and let it go easily if you don't get it	4	Say yes, but say or show that you prefer not to
Ask in a clear, polite way for what you want, but take no for an answer without resisting	5	Say no tentatively (e.g., that you would rather not), but give in easily if the other person persists
Ask in a confident manner for what you want, but take no for an answer without resisting	6	Say no in a confident manner, but be prepared to give in or negotiate if the other person persists
Ask in a confident manner for what you want, and resist if the other person says no (e.g., by negotiating or asking again)	7	Say no in a confident manner, and resist giving in or negotiating (at least at first) even if the other person persists
Ask clearly and strongly for what you want, and resist if the other person says no	8	Say no clearly and strongly, and resist giving in or negotiating (at least at first) even if the other person persists
Ask clearly and strongly for what you want, and keep asking, negotiating, or trying to convince the other person if they say no	9	Say no clearly and strongly, resist giving in, and keep trying to convince the other person to take no for an answer
Ask clearly and strongly for what you want, insist, and do not accept no for an answer	10	Say no clearly and strongly, and refuse to give in.

FACTORS TO CONSIDER IN DETERMINING YOUR LEVEL OF INTENSITY

While there isn't a precise, scientific way to determine with perfect accuracy the most effective level of intensity for a given situation, DBT proposes ten factors that can be considered to help you make this decision. For each of these factors that are present, you raise your level of intensity accordingly. We will outline the factors to consider here and provide an example below to illustrate how to apply this approach.

1. **ABILITY:** Does the other person actually have the ability to give you what you're asking for?

2. **PRIORITIES:** Consider how the goals and priorities you have identified might inform your level of intensity. If your objective or self-respect goal is the highest priority, consider raising your intensity; if your relationship goal is the highest priority, though, consider lowering your intensity.

3. **SELF-RESPECT:** Will asking strengthen your sense of self-respect or help you feel more capable and effective?

4. **RIGHTS:** Do you have the right to what you want according to any law or universal moral principle? In other words, would just about everyone agree that you are entitled to it?

5. **AUTHORITY:** Are you in a position of authority relative to the other person?

6. **APPROPRIATENESS TO THE RELATIONSHIP:** Given the nature of your relationship with this person, is it appropriate to ask for what you want?

7. **IMPACT ON LONG-TERM RELATIONSHIP:** Will asking for what you want help the relationship in the long term (even if it might be uncomfortable or create tension in the short term)? Or is it more likely to give you what you want in the short term at the expense of the longer-term relationship?

8. **BALANCE:** Do you give at least as much as you get? Is there balance in the relationship across time?

9. **THE FACTS:** Do you have all the relevant facts that you need in order to make this request? Have you done whatever research might be necessary?

10. **TIMING:** Is this a good time to ask the other person? Are they likely to say yes right now, or are there any reasons why now might not be the best time to ask?

Example: You are considering asking for a raise at work after several years at your current salary. *For each factor that indicates a higher level of intensity, we will note it with a +1. We will add these up at the end.*

1. **ABILITY:** Your employer is able to give you a raise. **+1.**

2. **PRIORITIES:** Let's assume the objective is your highest priority. **+1.**

3. **SELF-RESPECT:** Asking will strengthen your sense of self-respect. **+1.**

4. **RIGHTS:** You don't have the "right" to a raise according to any law or universal moral principle.

5. **AUTHORITY:** You are definitely not in a position of authority relative to your employer.

6. **APPROPRIATENESS TO THE RELATIONSHIP:** It is appropriate for an employee to ask an employer for a raise. **+1.**

7. **IMPACT ON LONG-TERM RELATIONSHIP:** It seems likely the relationship will suffer in the long term if you don't ask for a raise that you believe you deserve. **+1.**

8. **BALANCE:** You give a lot in this relationship, as you work hard at your job. **+1.**

9. **THE FACTS:** You have done your research by speaking to colleagues in similar positions so you know the raise you're requesting is reasonable. **+1.**

10. **TIMING:** You know your boss is under a lot of pressure at work right now and is dealing with some family stressors, so it's not great timing.

As you can see, when we add up all the factors that are present, we come to a total of 7. Look back at the list of levels of intensity in the table on page 156: 7 corresponds to "Ask in a confident manner for what you want, and resist if the other person says no (e.g., by negotiating or asking again)."

One note when it comes to determining your level of intensity: your Wise Mind is crucial in this process. The approach we have outlined is a helpful way of getting into the right ballpark, but the reality is not as straightforward as simply adding 1 + 1—so trust your intuition if you land at a Level 7, but your gut tells you that it would be most effective to knock it up or down a notch. Additionally, in some situations, one factor should be weighed more heavily, potentially even to the point of outweighing all the others. For example, if you know your boss just had a death in the family, timing alone is probably enough to outweigh all the other factors; you will likely decide to postpone asking for that raise. Let these factors help you get in the right ballpark, and use your Wise Mind to determine more precisely what level of intensity will be most effective.

Finally, we have presented all the above in the context of making a request of another person. To determine the level of intensity when you don't want to agree to a request from someone else, simply consider the reverse for each of the factors (e.g., "Am I able to give the other person what they want?" If not, add +1 to the intensity of saying no).

EXERCISE: *Clarifying Interpersonal Goals and Priorities*

In this exercise, you will practice identifying and prioritizing among your objective, relationship goal, and self-respect goal several times over the coming week. You will also consider the ways in which your goals might come in conflict with one another so that you are better prepared to act based on your priorities.

INSTRUCTIONS

Use the worksheet on page 163 to complete this exercise. If you do not face any challenging or emotional interpersonal situations this week, you can practice using examples from the past, issues that you anticipate coming up in the future, or even everyday interactions that are not particularly challenging or emotional (e.g., asking your roommate to pick something up from the grocery store). Even in these everyday interactions, you can consider Objectives Effectiveness, Relationship Effectiveness, and Self-Respect Effectiveness!

1. At least three times over the coming week, choose an interpersonal situation to practice clarifying your goals and priorities. Briefly describe just the facts of the situation.

2. Identify your objective. What is the result or outcome that you want from this discussion? What do you want to ask for, say no to, or express? What will help you bring about this outcome?

3. Identify your relationship goal. How do you want the other person to feel about you based on how you behave in this interaction? What do you need to do to achieve this goal? For example, "I want this person to continue liking me, so I need to make sure not to start criticizing or raising my voice."

4. Identify your self-respect goal. How do you want to feel about yourself based on how you behave in this interaction? What do you need to do (or not do) to achieve this goal? For example, "I want to feel proud of myself for not losing my temper, so I need to have a plan for how to cope if I start feeling angry."

5. Considering the specific objective, relationship, and self-respect goals you have identified, which one is your top Wise Mind priority in this situation? Which comes second, and third? Consider these questions:

    a. If the only way I could achieve my objective would be to sacrifice the relationship goal, would I do it?

    b. If the only way to achieve my objective would be to sacrifice my self-respect goal, would I do it?

    c. If the only way to achieve my relationship goal would be to sacrifice my self-respect goal, would I do it?

6. Some of your goals may align. Others will conflict with one another. For example, a relationship goal of keeping the other person happy with you may conflict with a self-respect goal of standing up for yourself by saying no to an unwanted request. Are there any ways in which you see your objective, relationship goal, and/or self-respect goal potentially coming into conflict with one another? If so, describe how in the space provided.

7. Finally, given the priorities you identified in Step 5, what would you need to do in order to act based on Wise Mind if your goals do come in conflict with one another?

It is not uncommon for someone to say, "I don't have a relationship goal (or self-respect goal) in this situation!" While the relationship or your self-respect may be less important than your objective in a given interaction, we actually always have goals in each of these categories—don't ignore them just because they are a lower priority!

For example, if you have to call your internet service provider because your Wi-Fi isn't working, it may not be a high priority to have the customer service representative like you. That said, assuming you can get your internet up and running again either way, would you prefer to have a pleasant interaction with the representative and hang up knowing that they enjoyed speaking with you, or would you rather act aggressively and know that you were unpleasant to deal with? Most of us would choose the former, achieving our objective *and* our relationship and self-respect goals. If you left out any of the goals above, go back now and consider what those would be.

CLARIFYING INTERPERSONAL GOALS AND PRIORITIES PRACTICE WORKSHEET

Situation: _____

Objective: _____

Relationship goal: _____

Self-respect goal: _____

1. **First priority (circle one):**
   OBJECTIVE   RELATIONSHIP GOAL   SELF-RESPECT GOAL

2. **Second priority (circle one):**
   OBJECTIVE   RELATIONSHIP GOAL   SELF-RESPECT GOAL

3. **Third priority (circle one):**
   OBJECTIVE   RELATIONSHIP GOAL   SELF-RESPECT GOAL

4. Are there any ways in which I see my objective coming in conflict with my relationship goal and/or self-respect goal? Are there any ways in which I see my relationship goal and self-respect goal coming in conflict?

   _____

   _____

   _____

   _____

5. How can I act based on my Wise Mind priorities if my goals do come in conflict with one another? _____

   _____

   _____

   _____

   _____

EXERCISE: *Practice Communicating at Different Levels of Intensity*

In this exercise, you will practice expressing yourself at varying levels of intensity. Many people struggle to communicate across the full range of options; the goal here is to broaden your repertoire so that you aren't limited to just a few levels of intensity!

INSTRUCTIONS

1. Choose a recent or ongoing interpersonal situation that brings up unwanted emotions (tip: you can use one of the situations you chose for the previous exercise).

2. Consider what you want from the other person (your objective) in this situation. For the purpose of this exercise, don't worry if it is something that you think is unrealistic or that you wouldn't actually express.

3. Using the table on page 156, practice expressing what you want at each of the levels of intensity. Practice each level of intensity *out loud*, so you can actually hear your own voice at each one. Don't be surprised if you feel uncomfortable at several levels! Although some of the levels will likely be inappropriate or ineffective for the situation you have chosen, practice each one anyway. The goal is to better understand and get comfortable communicating across the range of intensity, not to find the right one for this situation.

4. For extra credit, close your eyes and imagine that you are in the situation right now. Picture the other person, hear their voice, and imagine them resisting or pushing back in response when you ask (or when you say no to their request).

5. For further practice, choose at least two more situations and go through Steps 1 through 4. Try to come up with at least one situation in which you are making a request (the left column in the table on page 156) and at least one in which you are considering saying no to someone else's request (the right column in the table).

People often assume that to communicate at a higher level of intensity requires being aggressive or rude. The goal is to be assertive, though, not aggressive; you can be firm without bullying or intimidating the other person! If you think you might have approached the higher levels of intensity this way, go back again and instead try to express yourself in a way that is clear, direct, and unwavering rather than hostile.

EXERCISE: *Determine the Effective Level of Intensity*

Now that you are more comfortable expressing yourself across the full range of levels of intensity, all that remains is to learn how to determine the most effective level for any situation! In this exercise, you will practice this skill by applying it to a current situation in your own life.

INSTRUCTIONS

1. Choose a recent or ongoing interpersonal situation that brings up unwanted emotions, and identify what you want from the other person (your objective) in this situation. Feel free to use one of the situations you chose for a previous exercise in this chapter.

2. Consider each of the factors for determining level of intensity using the worksheet on the next page. Write a "+1" to the right of each factor that is present in the situation you have chosen. If you are uncertain whether a given factor is present, we would recommend erring on the side of caution and not adding a +1. Keep in mind, this doesn't mean that you will make your request at a low level of intensity; it simply means that you are not increasing the level one more degree. Additionally, any underestimation will be corrected when you adjust the final intensity based on Wise Mind!

3. Add up the total, and identify the corresponding level of intensity in the table on page 156. Check in with your Wise Mind to confirm if this seems to be an effective level of intensity (even if it would feel uncomfortable!). Adjust up or down as necessary.

Being more strategic about what level of intensity you use will help you get more of what you want as well as protect your relationships and your self-respect!

FACTORS FOR DETERMINING LEVEL OF INTENSITY	+1 IF YES:
ABILITY: Does the other person actually have the ability to give you what you're asking for?	
PRIORITIES: Consider how the goals and priorities you have identified might inform your level of intensity. If your objective or self-respect goal is the highest priority, consider raising your intensity; if your relationship goal is the highest priority, consider lowering your intensity.	
SELF-RESPECT: Will asking strengthen your sense of self-respect or help you feel more capable and effective?	
RIGHTS: Do you have the right to what you want according to any law or universal moral principle? In other words, would just about everyone agree that you are entitled to it?	
AUTHORITY: Are you in a position of authority relative to the other person?	
APPROPRIATENESS TO THE RELATIONSHIP: Given the nature of your relationship with this person, is it appropriate to ask for what you want?	
IMPACT ON LONG-TERM RELATIONSHIP: Will asking for what you want help the relationship in the long term? Or is it more likely to give you what you want in the short term at the expense of the longer-term relationship?	
BALANCE: Do you give at least as much as you get? Is there balance in the relationship across time?	
THE FACTS: Do you have all the relevant facts that you need in order to make this request? Have you done whatever research might be necessary?	
TIMING: Is this a good time to ask the other person? Are they likely to say yes right now, or are there any reasons why now might not be the best time to ask?	
TOTAL	
Effective level of intensity (including any adjustments for Wise Mind)	

Get More of What You Want in Your Relationships

WEEK 11

Last week we introduced the three areas of effectiveness to consider in any interpersonal situation: Objectives, Relationship, and Self-Respect. Identifying your goals and priorities in these areas sets the stage for communicating effectively, but it is just the first step—you have to actually have the conversation! This chapter will focus on strategies for maximizing the likelihood that you get what you want in any situation—in other words, how you can communicate in a way that increases your Objectives Effectiveness. The acronym for these skills is DEAR MAN.

DEAR: The Script (or, What to Say)

When we ask for something we want from another person—for example, a favor, an apology, or a change in their behavior—there are two types of pitfalls that are most likely to get in the way. The first is that we often don't clearly communicate what we're asking for, why we're asking for it, or why the other person would want to consider agreeing to it. Clarity is most effective, but instead we beat around the bush, assume the other person knows how we feel (or that we know how they feel!), and ultimately don't spell things out in a way that makes our request crystal clear.

The second pitfall is that we often communicate in a way that feels (or is!) judgmental and critical. For example, we say things like "You shouldn't have done that" or "How could you say that," and when we are deep into Emotion Mind, we may say much harsher things than that! Rather than achieving what we want, these types of comments usually just bring about defensiveness and attacks in return.

Our first set of communication strategies are intended to help you avoid these pitfalls by (1) increasing the clarity of what you're asking for, and (2) decreasing the likelihood of defensiveness or attacks from the other person. Think of these as an assertiveness outline or script—by following this structure and including the following four steps, you will express what you want more effectively and increase the likelihood that you get what you want. The acronym for this first set of skills is DEAR:

+ **D**ESCRIBE THE FACTS

+ **E**XPRESS HOW YOU FEEL

+ **A**SSERT YOURSELF

+ **R**EINFORCE THE OTHER PERSON

DESCRIBE

The first step is to make it clear to the other person what you want to talk about—in other words, what circumstances you are responding to. Describe just the facts that you directly observed, and avoid judgments, opinions, and generalizations. For example, say, "You have canceled on me the last three times we made plans" as opposed to "You're inconsiderate" or "You always bail on me."

EXPRESS

Don't assume that the other person knows how you feel, or that they will figure it out! Continuing with the example above, you could say, "This makes me worry that you don't want to spend time with me." You might think that your friend knows how their repeated cancelations make you feel, when the reality is that they are just as likely to assume you are angry at them or that you actually don't mind. Expressing your feelings helps the other person understand what is important to you about the situation. A word of caution, though: don't abandon your nonjudgmental stance when you express your feelings and opinions! Judgments are likely to derail the entire conversation.

ASSERT

Even if you do an A+ job of describing the situation and expressing your-self, don't make the mistake of assuming that the other person now knows what you want. Instead, ask for exactly what you want (or clearly say no), without being vague or leaving the other person to connect the dots. Think about our example: if you started with "You have canceled on me the last three times we made plans and this makes me worry that you don't want to spend time with me" and stop there, the other person might think you want reassurance that they do want to spend time with you, that you want an apology, or that you want an explanation for why they keep canceling. Be explicit so there is no guessing needed: for example, "I want you to show up when we make plans in the future. Will you?" The point here is not to be aggressive though—*ask* for what you want, don't demand it or tell someone what they *should* do or *must* do.

REINFORCE

Reinforcement in this context refers to "rewarding" the other person for responding in the way that you want (i.e., positive reinforcement). In other words, tell the other person what is in it for them! If this sounds like manipulation, don't worry; the idea here is to make the interaction more positive for *both* people. Often, we only emphasize why we want something, which isn't very focused on the other person. With the Reinforce skill, you think about the other person too and highlight why they would want to agree.

It can be difficult to identify positive consequences to reinforce the other person. Often it requires knowing them and what they might find rewarding. Consider if there are any positive consequences that will result naturally or automatically from the other person agreeing to your request (e.g., "I think we'll both have fun and it will make our friendship stronger"). Even a simple expression of gratitude can be reinforcing! (e.g., "I'd really appreciate it," or "It would mean a lot to me.")

Lastly, keep in mind that communicating positive consequences is generally more effective than relying on threats or punishments for creating lasting behavior change—not to mention that focusing on negative consequences can damage relationships. That said, stating negative consequences can of course be effective if they are true or when positive reinforcement doesn't succeed (e.g., "If you continue canceling our plans, I am going to stop making plans with you.")

MAN: How to Use Your DEAR Script

So you're all excited to use your new DEAR skills. You know exactly the situation that calls for them, you write out your script and practice it with a friend, and then you go in for the real-life conversation and . . . your request gets shot down. Not only that, but the other person turns the conversation around, and it ends up being about something entirely different from what you were hoping.

How can you still be effective in trying to achieve the objective you started with? This is where the MAN skills come in. If the DEAR skills provide the script for *what* to say in asserting yourself, think of the MAN skills as strategies for *how* to assert yourself when the objective is a high priority—including how to respond effectively if the other person doesn't agree or react the way you hoped. The MAN skills are as follows:

+ (STAY) **M**INDFUL OF YOUR OBJECTIVE

+ **A**PPEAR CONFIDENT

+ **N**EGOTIATE

(STAY) MINDFUL

It is really easy to get sidetracked from your "Assert," especially if the other person changes the subject or criticizes you. To get what you want, though, it's crucial that you stay Mindful of your objective. Two strategies that will help you maintain focus are **ignoring attacks** and acting like a **broken record.**

Ignoring attacks means literally ignoring when the other person says anything that might knock you off course from your objective (e.g., attacks, threats, "but you do the same thing," etc.). Even if they say something that you want to address, ignore it for now; you can always come back and DEAR MAN that comment later, once you have (hopefully) achieved your original objective for this conversation. By ignoring attacks, you maintain control of the conversation. Otherwise, it becomes a discussion about their comment rather than your objective.

So what are you to do when the other person attacks or changes the subject? Act like a **broken record**! Simply reiterate the request (or say no) over and over again—just like a literal broken record that is repeating the same lines in a song. You might repeat your entire DEAR script, or a specific piece of it. This strategy prevents you from getting sidetracked, and takes off any pressure you might feel to come up with new ways to make your request—which is particularly challenging when your emotions are running high. It also increases the likelihood that the other person eventually responds to your request (even if it doesn't guarantee that they agree to it), since any efforts to take the conversation in another direction lead right back to the same broken-record response.

It is important to keep your tone of voice even and calm when you use this skill. We are often tempted to raise our voices, emphasize certain words, or otherwise communicate something through our tone when we repeat ourselves—all of which run the risk of eliciting defensiveness or attacks from the other person. Let your steadfastness and refusal to be knocked off course do the talking instead.

Here is what acting like a broken record might look like:

YOU: [start with the following DEAR script] When you said last night that I don't do my fair share of the chores, it hurt my feelings and made me think you don't recognize everything that I do. I would like for you to apologize for saying that, and to acknowledge the things that I do. The truth is that I'll be likely to do even more if you acknowledge what I already do and I feel like my efforts are appreciated.

THEM: Well, you *don't* do your fair share of the chores. I shouldn't need to acknowledge the few things you do so you'll pull your weight!

YOU: We can certainly talk about how we divide up the chores. That said, it hurts my feelings when you say that, and I want you to apologize and acknowledge the things I do. I'll be more likely to take on more if you do that.

THEM: I can't believe you're turning this around on me. You don't do your fair share, and somehow I'm the bad guy.

YOU: Like I said, we can talk about how we divide the chores. It does hurt my feelings when you say that though, and I would like you to apologize and acknowledge the things I do.

As you can see, ignoring attacks and acting like a broken record are not easy! The other person may very well not appreciate it. If the objective is a priority for you, though—especially if it is a higher priority than your relationship goal—then it is worth considering these strategies even if the other person won't like it.

APPEAR CONFIDENT

Act in a manner that communicates that your opinions and desires deserve to be taken seriously. For example, stand or sit up straight, make strong eye contact, and speak in a confident tone of voice. This skill is about using nonverbal behavior to increase the likelihood that you get what you want. Picture yourself making the same request in two different ways: in one scenario you are looking at the floor, stammering, speaking softly, and generally acting like you are inconveniencing the other person; in the other, you are standing with confident posture, looking the other person in the eye, and asking for what you want in a clear and matter-of-fact manner. Which version is more likely to achieve what you're asking for? It's worth noting that appearing confident is effective even when you make your initial DEAR statement—not only if the other person says no.

NEGOTIATE

Lastly, be prepared to negotiate. When the other person doesn't give you what you want, there is no shortage of negotiation strategies that you can use. Consider offering to do something in exchange, suggest alternatives, or accept less than your full request. One helpful approach is to "turn the tables" by handing the problem over to the other person—in other words, get them involved in generating solutions so that you aren't the only one making suggestions. For example, you could say, "We don't seem to be finding a solution here. I need something to change—can you think of any options I haven't considered?"

One final note: no matter how interpersonally skillful you are, there is unfortunately no way to guarantee that you will achieve your goals in a given situation. After all, you can't control how the other person will respond! For this reason, we recommend that you evaluate based on your approach rather than the outcome. If you have used your skills effectively, give yourself an A+, even if you don't get the result you wanted! Over time, you will achieve your goals more often by sticking to these strategies.

EXERCISE: *Constructing a DEAR Script*

In this exercise, you will practice constructing a DEAR script using an example from a recent or ongoing personal situation. As you go through each step, make sure to be concise! A common mistake is to go into an unnecessary amount of detail, and the other person is likely to stop listening to what you're saying. A full DEAR script is typically just a few sentences, not several paragraphs.

INSTRUCTIONS

1. Choose an interpersonal situation that brings up unwanted emotions. Briefly describe the facts of the situation using the worksheet on page 176.

2. Identify your objective. What is the result or outcome that you want from this discussion? For example, getting the other person to agree to something, saying no, or obtaining an apology.

3. For this step and the remaining steps, write out the actual words you will say to the other person, as though you are writing a script for yourself. First, Describe relevant facts. What exactly are you responding to? What made you want to communicate something? Remember to be objective and nonjudgmental.

4. Next, Express how you feel about these facts. Don't assume the other person should know! Include specific emotion words and/or your opinion about the situation, while remaining nonjudgmental.

5. Assert yourself. Ask for what you want (or say no), clearly and explicitly. Again, the other person can't read your mind, so don't tiptoe around actually asking for what you want.

6. Reinforce the other person. Tell them why they would want to agree to what you Asserted. Emphasize rewards rather than punishments.

continued

SITUATION: _____

OBJECTIVE: _____

DESCRIBE: _____

_____

Example: "When you said I don't do my fair share of the chores . . ."

EXPRESS: _____

_____

Example: "I felt hurt. I worry you don't notice everything I do."

ASSERT: _____

_____

Example: "I would like for you to apologize for saying that, and to acknowledge the things that I do."

REINFORCE: _____

_____

Example: "The truth is that I'll be likely to do even more if you acknowledge what I already do and I feel like my efforts are appreciated."

Once you have completed all the components of your DEAR script, review your responses and edit as necessary to increase their effectiveness. Be sure to use your Wise Mind as you do this, as Emotion Mind is liable to make your script more aggressive, judgmental, or avoidant! Lastly, practice reading your script out loud or role-play it with a friend. Although this is often uncomfortable at first, it will get easier with repetition. When the time comes for the real conversation, you will be more likely to stick to the script *and* sound more natural doing it.

EXERCISE: *Incorporating the MAN Skills*

In this exercise, you are going to practice incorporating the MAN skills into a DEAR script.

INSTRUCTIONS

1. Review your objective and DEAR script from the previous exercise.

2. Identify what you can do to stay Mindful of your objective. Are there any specific attacks, threats, or distracting comments that the other person is likely to make? While it isn't possible to predict everything, it can be helpful to identify likely responses and prepare for them. How could you act like a broken record? Would you repeat your full DEAR script, or just a portion of it? Is there some other response you want to use in your broken record?

3. Consider steps you can take to Appear confident. What happens to your body language, posture, facial expression, eye contact, or tone of voice when you feel anxious or insecure? What would it look like to Act Opposite to anxiety? How would you avoid saying anything that sounds tentative or uncertain (e.g., "I'm so sorry to bother you with this, but . . .")?

4. Prepare specific Negotiation strategies to use. Ask Wise Mind: What would I be willing to give in order to get what I want? It is harder to negotiate effectively on the fly—especially when emotions are running high—so it is helpful to have a "Plan B" (and C!) in mind in case negotiation is needed. Write down specific statements you can use to suggest these options.

continued

5. Practice! Here are three options:

   a. The most effective approach is to have another person role-play the conversation with you. Provide some context beforehand, and tell them the specific types of attacks or responses you want them to make in the other person's role.

   b. If role-playing isn't possible, practice in front of a mirror or while recording yourself, imagining the other person's responses. This will also give you a useful perspective on your Appear confident strategies.

   c. Close your eyes and imagine yourself in the conversation, as though it is happening right now. Say your parts of the conversation out loud.

You might feel tempted to skip Step 5 once you have written everything out above. Don't! It isn't enough to know what you plan to say or do, especially because emotions are likely to interfere with sticking to the plan if you haven't rehearsed it. Actual behavioral practice is the most effective way to both improve at these skills as well as increase the likelihood that you use them.

ATTACKS AND OTHER COMMENTS I WILL IGNORE *(e.g., When they call me too emotional; when they say "it's always something"; if they threaten to walk out.)*

_____

_____

_____

BROKEN-RECORD PLAN *(e.g., Repeat my full DEAR script; repeat my Reinforce; keep saying, "You haven't responded to what I requested. I would appreciate a response, please.")*

_____

_____

STRATEGIES FOR APPEARING CONFIDENT *(e.g., Make eye contact, maintain confident voice tone.)*

_____

_____

NEGOTIATION STRATEGIES AND STATEMENTS *(e.g., Offer to work on the thing I know they want if they agree to this; tell them I can accept that they won't do X if they're willing to do Y.)*

_____

_____

_____

EXERCISE: *DEAR MAN Practice*

Now that you have tried out each of the DEAR MAN skills, it's time to practice! For this exercise, you will use DEAR MAN several times this week. You can use these skills in everyday situations, even if they aren't necessary. For example, you can even use DEAR MAN in ordering your morning coffee ("I've been tired all morning and would love to feel more alert. Can I please have a large iced coffee with skim milk and sugar? I would really appreciate it!")

INSTRUCTIONS

1. Three times over the coming week, choose a situation to practice DEAR MAN. If a new situation doesn't arise that obviously requires these skills, consider ongoing situations in which they could be helpful (e.g., something your parents regularly do that annoys you; something you've been avoiding telling your partner that you want to change in the relationship). As we mentioned earlier, you can also practice in everyday situations. Last but not least, if you don't have any social interactions on a given day, you can complete this exercise regarding past interactions as well.

2. Use the worksheet on the next page to implement the skills you learned in the first two exercises of this chapter for each of these situations. Review the instructions to those exercises if necessary. As you will be practicing several times, download copies of this template (use the QR code on page 208), or write out the steps on a separate piece of paper.

3. Don't just write out the steps—put them into action!

Although we recommend including all of the steps of DEAR MAN as you practice, it is worth noting that not every situation requires Describing and Expressing. As you can tell from our example of ordering coffee above, at times it is perfectly fine to just skip right to your Assert! Assume that it will generally be most effective to use the full DEAR script though, and use your Wise Mind if you are considering leaving out any steps.

SITUATION: _____

_____

OBJECTIVE: _____

_____

DESCRIBE: _____

_____

EXPRESS: _____

_____

ASSERT: _____

_____

REINFORCE: _____

_____

ATTACKS/COMMENTS TO IGNORE: _____

_____

BROKEN-RECORD PLAN: _____

_____

APPEAR CONFIDENT STRATEGIES: _____

_____

NEGOTIATION STRATEGIES AND STATEMENTS: _____

_____

Protect Your Relationships with Others . . . and with Yourself

As you learned in Week 10, communicating effectively includes skillfully asking for what you want as well as doing so in a way that protects your relationship and your self-respect. The DEAR MAN skills you learned last week are just the first piece of that puzzle. This week, we will complete the picture by introducing the skills for Relationship Effectiveness and Self-Respect Effectiveness. These strategies maximize the likelihood that even as you try to get what you want, you walk away from difficult conversations with your relationships and your self-respect secure—and hopefully improved!

Increasing Relationship Effectiveness: The GIVE Skills

The concept of Relationship Effectiveness probably comes as no surprise: we all tend to communicate differently when our relationship with the other person is important to us than when it isn't. For example, think about the difference between how you would ask for something from a close friend versus from a telephone customer service agent that you will never speak to again. Although you may be polite and friendly to the customer service agent, you might also be willing to push harder to get what you want than you would in speaking to your friend. It makes sense: if you care about a relationship and how the other person feels about you, you need to communicate in a way that reflects that.

You might have wondered, "Aren't the DEAR MAN skills I learned last week likely to upset the other person?" After all, it's hard to imagine that anyone would enjoy being on the other side of the broken-record technique! This is where the Relationship Effectiveness skills, also called the GIVE skills, come into play. While these need to be considered in any interaction, they are particularly necessary when your relationship goal is a high priority. Think of these skills as stylistic elements that balance your efforts to get what you want while keeping the other person liking you. While the DEAR skills provide the script for what to say, the following four GIVE skills are strategies for how to deliver that script in a way that protects your relationship. The GIVE skills are as follows:

+ (BE) **G**ENTLE

+ (ACT) **I**NTERESTED

+ **V**ALIDATE

+ (USE AN) **E**ASY MANNER

(BE) GENTLE

Being Gentle is kind of like the Golden Rule: "Do unto others as you would have them do unto you." In this context, though, this statement refers to what is effective rather than a moral imperative. In other words, if you want to maintain a good relationship with someone, it is crucial to be nice and respectful—especially in difficult conversations. Don't attack the other person, verbally or physically. Don't threaten negative consequences to get what you want, or deliberately try to "manipulate" someone into complying. Don't communicate in a judgmental way, and don't act in a way that the other person is likely to experience as disrespectful, condescending, or dismissive. Just as you presumably don't appreciate being attacked, threatened, judged, or disrespected, it's safe to assume that nobody else does either!

(ACT) INTERESTED

Acting in a way that indicates you care about the other person's emotions and opinions, *especially* during a sensitive discussion, goes a long way toward building a strong relationship. We can get so caught up in our own feelings that we are not interested in the other person's point of view—or at the very least, we don't show that we are! Verbally, the main way to act Interested is to ask questions. Dive into understanding the other person's perspective. Don't assume that you know what their opinions or intentions are, especially if you're assuming they were selfish or malicious! Also avoid interrupting or changing topics. Nonverbally, acting Interested includes facing the other person, looking them in the eye as they speak, and nodding or making sounds of approval occasionally.

VALIDATE

To Validate means to communicate that you understand the other person's experience and why they felt, thought, or acted as they did. Validation is a relationship-improving superpower! It shows that you care about the other person and their point of view. While always important, validation is especially valuable during a disagreement, because it shifts the focus from who is "right" or winning the argument to a mutual effort to understand and resolve the problem.

To be clear, validation does not mean you need to agree with the other person, apologize, or say that something makes sense to you when it doesn't. It is not just "lip service"! Rather, the goal is to thoughtfully figure out what you *can* understand. In trying to find what you can Validate, consider the facts of the situation ("Yes, that driver really did run that red light"), the other person's emotions ("I understand why you felt hurt when

I said you don't care about my feelings"), their thoughts or interpretations ("I can understand your point of view, even though I disagree"), and their actions or urges ("It makes sense that you would want to avoid that person"). There is always *something* understandable in a person's response to any situation—it is your job to find it! If you truly cannot make sense of any part of the other person's reactions, express your desire to understand and ask questions. In other words, use your act Interested skill.

There are six "levels" of validation that you can use, with each level being a stronger form of validation than the one that comes before it.

1. PAY ATTENTION: Show that you are listening through your facial expression (e.g., eye contact, nodding occasionally), body language (e.g., facing the other person), and actions (e.g., not multitasking or looking at your phone).

2. REFLECT BACK: Repeat back (or paraphrase) what the other person said to communicate that you were listening. Do this in a way that shows you are trying to understand, not that you agree or disagree, or approve or disapprove. For example, "Got it—when I didn't text you back sooner, you thought I was ignoring you."

3. "READ MINDS": Figure out what the other person hasn't explicitly said about their thoughts or feelings and verbalize it. Consider what they *did* say, your knowledge of the person, their actions, and their nonverbal behaviors (e.g., facial expression, posture, tone of voice). Be open to the possibility that you are reading the situation incorrectly, though. For example, "You seem really disappointed—is that right?"

4. UNDERSTAND BASED ON PERSONAL CONTEXT: Communicate that the other person's thoughts, emotions, or actions make sense based on their personal experiences. At this level you express that you understand *why* they think or feel the way they do, given their personal history (e.g., "I understand why you don't want to visit your parents, considering your relationship"), mental or physical state ("Of course you're anxious about the party; you have social anxiety"), or specific circumstances ("They said they would send a job offer by yesterday— I understand why you're afraid they changed their mind!").

5. **ACKNOWLEDGE WHAT IS VALID:** Communicate that the other person's reaction is understandable based on the situation, not only based on their personal context—in other words, that anyone might respond this way. At this level, you are saying, "Of course you feel this way—who wouldn't?" You can also Validate at this level by acting in a way that shows you understand and care—for example, giving a friend a hug or tissue if they are crying.

6. **SHOW EQUALITY:** Treat the other person as your equal. Don't treat them as helpless or fragile. Don't behave condescendingly or treat them as inferior. Be yourself, acting as you would with anyone else. For example, express your feelings rather than "walking on eggshells," acknowledge when you make a mistake, and expect as much of the other person as you would of anyone else (taking into account any genuine limitations). At this level, you are treating the other *person* as valid.

(USE AN) EASY MANNER

By approaching a difficult conversation in an easygoing manner, you send the message that the relationship isn't in danger, even if you disagree or dislike something the other person did. Smile, speak in a lighthearted tone, crack a joke, and relax your body language and facial expressions. Act in a way that communicates "this isn't the biggest deal, there is no reason to be alarmed" rather than "this is serious, we need to talk." Decreasing the tension also makes it more likely that the other person enjoys the discussion—and maybe even feels happy to give you what you want.

Increasing Self-Respect Effectiveness: The FAST Skills

The way you communicate has the potential to impact how you feel about yourself. For example, losing your temper and yelling at a friend might cause you to feel shame and guilt, whereas communicating calmly even though you're angry might leave you feeling proud of yourself. Additionally, your self-respect can be affected if you agree to do something (or not do something) that violates your values. For example, someone might ask their accountant to cheat on their taxes. Assuming this is against the accountant's values, agreeing—for example, out of discomfort saying no or fear of upsetting the client—would decrease the accountant's self-respect, whereas saying no and sticking to their values would increase it. The Self-Respect Effectiveness skills help ensure that, at a minimum, you don't end a conversation feeling guilty or ashamed; ideally, you will even feel a greater sense of pride and self-confidence. While these skills need to be considered in any interaction, they are particularly important when your self-respect goal is a high priority.

Like the GIVE skills, the Self-Respect Effectiveness skills are incorporated into your DEAR script to balance trying to get what you want with maintaining your self-respect. The acronym for these skills is FAST:

+ (BE) **F**AIR

+ (NO) **A**POLOGIES

+ **S**TICK TO YOUR VALUES

+ (BE) **T**RUTHFUL

(BE) FAIR

It is important to be fair, both to yourself and to the other person. If you consistently give in to other people's wishes and never say no, it is hard to respect yourself. Similarly, if you disproportionately take-take-take in your relationships or take advantage of other people, that will also affect how you feel about yourself. The key is finding a balance of taking care of both yourself and the other person. Consider whether you give as much as you take in the relationship, balance standing up for yourself with letting the other person get their way, and validate both your own feelings and the other person's.

(NO) APOLOGIES

Don't make apologies that aren't warranted or effective. Apologies are appropriate when you have done something that violates your own values. Additionally, at times it can be effective to apologize for the sake of a relationship even if you didn't intend harm or to do something against your values. Apologies indicate that you have done something "wrong," though, so saying sorry when it is not warranted can chip away at your self-respect over time. Don't say sorry simply for wanting something, saying no, or disagreeing. Also don't apologize for your identity, your personality traits, or your beliefs and values. Finally, even if an apology is called for, don't apologize repeatedly for the same thing. In addition to eroding your self-respect, excessive apologizing can irritate the other person and damage the relationship, too.

STICK TO YOUR VALUES

You may be tempted at times to compromise on your values to get what you want, protect a relationship, or gain someone's approval. However, habitually hiding your true beliefs or repeatedly saying or doing things that you consider immoral can undermine your self-respect. Stand up for your values, be honest about what you believe, and say no when you are asked or pressured to do something that you consider wrong. While there may be situations in which the relationship or your objective is so important that you are willing to compromise on your values, these are typically rare—make sure that doing so would be consistent with your Wise Mind.

(BE) TRUTHFUL

Finally, be honest rather than lying, exaggerating, or pretending to need help or support when you don't. There may be times when being dishonest may be effective in getting what you want, or when a "little white lie" may be in the best interest of a relationship. Consistent dishonesty is likely to eat away at your self-respect, though, as it is generally incompatible with acting in a way that leaves you feeling like a capable, effective person. This skill, like all of the FAST skills, is about balance.

Perhaps more than any of the other modules, it is often necessary to integrate all the Interpersonal Effectiveness skills in a single situation. You may need to clarify your goals and priorities, determine the appropriate level of intensity, and construct a DEAR script with a balance of MAN, GIVE, and FAST skills. In addition, you might need to regulate your emotions first using your Mindfulness, Emotion Regulation, and Distress Tolerance skills! You now have all the ingredients you need, though—all that's left to do is keep practicing and using the skills you have learned in this book. With enough practice, these skills will become second nature for you.

EXERCISE: *Validate in Your Day-to-Day Interactions*

Although validation is particularly important in a disagreement or a conversation that brings up strong emotions, you can practice it just about any time. Incorporating validation into your day-to-day interactions will improve your relationships, too! In this exercise, you will practice each of the levels of validation over the course of the week.

INSTRUCTIONS

1. Once per day over the coming week, choose a conversation in which to practice validation.

2. In each conversation, choose a specific level of validation to practice from the list on pages 185–186. For example, you may decide you are going to practice Level 1 ("pay attention") when you speak to a colleague or Level 5 ("acknowledge what is valid") when your partner complains about work.

3. Keep validating at this level throughout the conversation! Don't just do it once and stop there.

4. In the chart on the next page, record what level you practiced, how you did so, and any notes or observations about the experience. How did it feel to Validate? What did you notice about the other person's reactions? How did the conversation go?

5. Over the course of the week, be sure to practice each level of validation at least once.

As you get more comfortable with validation, we recommend practicing in conflicts and disagreements as well. One challenge is that in our eagerness to defend ourselves or express our own opinions, we often do not pause to first acknowledge what the other person has said. Instead, respond with validation first and only then go on to present your side of the argument. This can work wonders in defusing tension in difficult conversations.

continued

Exercise: Validate in Your Day-to-Day Interactions *continued*

DAY	SITUATION	HOW I VALIDATED	NOTES/ OBSERVATIONS

EXERCISE: *Practice the GIVE Skills*

In this exercise, you will practice incorporating the GIVE skills into a DEAR script. You will begin by identifying the relevant GIVE skills to use within a specific situation, then integrate your GIVE plans into the text of your DEAR script.

INSTRUCTIONS

1. Choose a recent or ongoing interpersonal situation that brings up unwanted emotions, in which your relationship goal is an important priority. Briefly describe the facts of the situation.

2. Consider which of the GIVE skills to incorporate and how:

   a. Are there any specific strategies you will use to be Gentle? Any attacks, threats, judgments, or disrespectful behaviors that you need to avoid?

   b. What questions will you ask to act Interested? How can you show the person you care about their viewpoint? What behaviors would demonstrate interest?

   c. Are there any Validating statements you can incorporate into your initial DEAR script? Although there is no way to predict everything the other person might say, is there anything you know about them or the situation that you can use to validate at Levels 4 or 5?

   d. How can you use an Easy manner and lighten the mood? (Note: this does not necessarily mean you have to lower the intensity of your Assert.) Should you use any skills beforehand to relax and ensure that you can act more lighthearted?

continued

3. Write out your DEAR script, keeping in mind your relationship goal and the GIVE skills you have decided to use.

4. Practice! Role-play the conversation with someone, practice in front of a mirror or while recording yourself, or close your eyes and imagine yourself having the conversation. Pay attention to your GIVE skills, in particular.

SITUATION: _____

RELATIONSHIP GOAL: _____

HOW I WILL INCORPORATE GIVE SKILLS

Strategies for being Gentle: _____

_____

Act Interested strategies and questions: _____

_____

Validation plans and statements: _____

_____

_____

Easy manner behaviors: _____

_____

DEAR SCRIPT (WITH GIVE SKILLS INCLUDED)

Describe: _____

_____

_____

Express: _____

_____

_____

Assert: _____

_____

_____

Reinforce: _____

_____

_____

The GIVE skills may appear fairly obvious; after all, who wouldn't agree that attacks and threats are damaging to a relationship, and that paying attention to the other person is a basic necessity if you want to protect the relationship? The challenge is often how to keep these strategies in mind when you need them, especially when Emotion Mind threatens to take the conversation in an ineffective direction. Use this exercise to get in the habit of planning ahead as well as to practice using these skills.

EXERCISE: *Putting It All Together: Incorporating the FAST Skills*

In this exercise, you are going to put together all of the Interpersonal Effectiveness skills you've learned these past three weeks by integrating the DEAR MAN, GIVE, and FAST skills and considering how to apply all of these in a single situation. Use the worksheet on page 196 to write out your answers. Review the instructions from any previous exercises for additional details if necessary.

INSTRUCTIONS

1. Choose a recent or ongoing interpersonal situation that brings up unwanted emotions. Briefly describe the facts of the situation.

2. Identify your objective, relationship goal, and self-respect goal, and rank your priorities among these. Consider any ways in which you see your goals potentially coming in conflict with one another, and plan how to act based on Wise Mind if this happens.

3. Consider your level of intensity using the worksheet on page 156.

4. Keeping in mind the balance of your priorities between your objective, relationship goal, and self-respect goal, consider which of the MAN, GIVE, and FAST skills to incorporate and how. Consult the instructions from the "Incorporating the MAN Skills" exercise last week and from the "Practice the GIVE Skills" exercise on page 191 as necessary. Regarding the FAST skills:

   a. Consider if you are being Fair to yourself and the other person. If not, how can you balance your feelings and theirs?

   b. Don't (over)Apologize. If you feel an urge to say sorry repeatedly or when it isn't warranted, what can you do instead?

    c. Stick to your values. If you are asked to do something inconsistent with your morals, or feel a desire to hide specific values or beliefs, how can you handle this in a way that is true to yourself?

    d. Be Truthful. If you feel an urge to lie or exaggerate, practice Opposite Action and be honest instead.

5. Write out your DEAR script, keeping in mind the level of intensity and the MAN, GIVE, and FAST skills you have decided to use.

6. Practice! Role-play the conversation with someone, practice in front of a mirror or while recording yourself, or close your eyes and imagine yourself having the conversation.

Until now, you have practiced the MAN, GIVE, and FAST skills separately. In most situations, however, it will be important to incorporate and balance skills from each of these categories. Ideally you will be able to achieve your objective, relationship goal, and self-respect goal! Additionally, each area of effectiveness can impact the others. For example, keeping the other person liking you is often helpful in getting what you want ("you catch more flies with honey than vinegar"); getting what you want can improve your self-respect; and in the long-term, acting in a way that enhances your self-respect can also enhance your relationships.

continued

GOALS AND PRIORITIES

SITUATION: _____

OBJECTIVE: _____

RELATIONSHIP GOAL: _____

SELF-RESPECT GOAL: _____

Rank your order of priorities.

1. First priority (circle one):

   OBJECTIVE   RELATIONSHIP GOAL   SELF-RESPECT GOAL

2. Second priority (circle one):

   OBJECTIVE   RELATIONSHIP GOAL   SELF-RESPECT GOAL

3. Third priority (circle one):

   OBJECTIVE   RELATIONSHIP GOAL   SELF-RESPECT GOAL

   How might my goals conflict with one another? How will I act based on my Wise Mind priorities if this occurs?

   _____

   _____

   _____

INTENSITY

Effective level of intensity (with adjustments for Wise Mind): _____

MAN, GIVE, AND FAST

Which MAN skills will I use and how? _____

_____

_____

Which GIVE skills will I use and how? _____

_____

_____

Which FAST skills will I use and how? _____

_____

_____

DEAR SCRIPT

DESCRIBE: _____

_____

EXPRESS: _____

_____

ASSERT: _____

_____

REINFORCE: _____

_____

APPENDIX

What Comes Next?

You've made it through all four modules—congratulations! We hope that you have found these tools helpful and that you are already incorporating them into your everyday life. You can look back at the targets you identified in the "Commit to Practicing DBT Skills" exercise on page 15 to check your progress. By now it should be clear why we think of DBT skills as "life skills" that can benefit everyone. So what comes next?

First and foremost, we strongly recommend that you continue practicing. You may find it helpful to go back and review specific chapters or exercises, or even to reread this entire book. You can download reusable copies of this book's worksheets by scanning the QR code on page 208. In fact, the "standard" in most DBT skills training groups is to complete two full rounds, learning all the skills twice. This can be helpful because you may have a completely different perspective on a skill the second time around once you are familiar with the other skills.

Additionally, as many situations require skills from several modules, you will be better able to understand how to integrate them when you review for the second time. For example, if someone makes a comment that brings up intense anger, you may need to start with your STOP skill (a Distress Tolerance skill), then Check the Facts (an Emotion Regulation skill) before ultimately using DEAR MAN, GIVE, and FAST to address the situation (Interpersonal Effectiveness skills). Whether you choose to reread or use a different approach to keep your skills fresh, ultimately the most important thing is that you continue practicing. Use your Problem Solving skills to come up with a plan that works for you!

To help with your skills use going forward, we have included several resources in the upcoming pages. The first is simply a list of all the DBT skills we covered in this book. Looking over this list can serve as a quick refresher of the skills you have learned. Additionally, if you are unsure what skill(s) to use in a given situation, looking through this list may help.

The second resource is a template for you to create your own "DBT Skills Cheat Sheet." This is a list of skills you find most helpful in a crisis, as well as behaviors that you want to make absolutely sure to avoid. This can be used hand in hand with your distress tolerance kit, and you might find it helpful to include a copy of it in your kit.

The third resource is a list of "The Five Options for Solving Any Problem." This can provide a helpful framework when thinking about how to approach any situation, as well as point you toward the relevant skills based on which option you choose.

Finally, we have included a list of additional resources as well, including DBT-related books, videos, podcasts, and online directories for finding a DBT therapist or program.

Now that you are familiar with the skills, you may be wondering if you would benefit from attending a DBT skills training group. We have attempted to present the skills in this book very similarly to how we teach them in our groups, *and* there are other DBT skills that we did not include in this book, as well as benefits to learning the skills in an interactive setting (e.g., the opportunity to ask questions, receive feedback, practice with others, and connect with others who may face similar challenges). In other words, we can't make a one-size-fits-all recommendation. There can certainly be additional benefits, and you may not personally find it necessary. We would recommend checking in with your Wise Mind to determine what would be most effective for you, or reaching out to a DBT therapist and talking to them about your specific situation.

Last but not least, if you are struggling to apply these skills consistently in your life; if you are suffering and feel like your life is an emotional hell; or if you struggle with BPD, self-harm, chronic suicide urges, or other impulsive behaviors, we strongly recommend that you seek a comprehensive DBT program. Comprehensive DBT is intended not only to help you learn DBT skills but also to apply them consistently in the contexts that you need them the most, as well as to address the specific challenges that you are personally facing. While we hope you have found this book helpful, no book can take the place of the personalized attention that a therapist can provide.

We hope that this book is only the beginning of your DBT journey! In our personal and professional experience, the benefits of reviewing, practicing, and using DBT skills only grow over time—even over the course of several years. We're confident that the more you utilize the tools and resources we've provided, the more you will be able to build your own personal Life Worth Living.

List of DBT Skills Covered in This Book

Mindfulness

+ The "What" skills: Observe, Describe, Participate
+ The "How" skills: Nonjudgmentally, One-Mindfully, Effectively
+ Wise Mind

Emotion Regulation

+ Understand and Label Your Emotions
+ Mindfulness of Current Emotions
+ Check the Facts
+ Opposite Action
+ Problem Solving
+ Accumulate Positive Emotions in the Short Term
+ Accumulate Positive Emotions in the Long Term
+ Build Mastery
+ Cope Ahead
+ PLEASE

Distress Tolerance

+ STOP
+ Distract with ACCEPTS
+ Self-Soothe
+ IMPROVE the moment
+ Pros and Cons
+ TIP
+ Radical Acceptance
+ Half-Smiling
+ Willing Hands
+ Turn the Mind

Interpersonal Effectiveness

+ Clarifying Goals and Priorities
+ Determining Level of Intensity When Asking for Something or Responding to a Request
+ DEAR MAN
+ GIVE
+ FAST

DBT Skills Cheat Sheet

Adapted from DBT PE Handout 3 in Treating Trauma in Dialectical Behavior Therapy: The DBT Prolonged Exposure Protocol (DBT PE) *by Melanie S. Harned*

Use this template to come up with a personalized crisis coping plan. In the first section, identify the skills you find most helpful in coping with intense emotions. In the second section, identify any problem behaviors that you want to avoid. Consider including a copy of this Cheat Sheet in your Distress Tolerance kit, as well as anywhere you are most likely to experience an emotional crisis.

Skills to use:

1. _____
2. _____
3. _____
4. _____
5. _____
6. _____
7. _____
8. _____
9. _____
10. _____

Problem behaviors to avoid:

1. _____
2. _____
3. _____
4. _____
5. _____
6. _____
7. _____
8. _____
9. _____
10. _____

The Five Options for Solving Any Problem

Inspired by Alejandra Linden's 6-Options Skill 1-Pager [adapted/modified from Linehan (2015) General Handout 1a]

A problem is an experience that causes painful emotions or makes you wish reality were different. It may be external, like something that happens to you, a relationship conflict, or an ongoing stressor. It may be internal, like unwanted thoughts, physical sensations, or body responses.

Whenever we have a problem in our lives, we have five options for how to deal with it.

1. **Change the problem.**

   a. Problem Solve. Figure out how to change the situation (fully or partly) or prevent a repeat of the problem.

   b. Act effectively. Use the emotion and do what your body is telling you to do, if the action would be helpful for you or your goals. Use skills (e.g., Interpersonal Effectiveness) as needed, too.

2. **Change how you think/feel about the problem.**

   a. Check the Facts. Confirm that your thoughts about the problem are accurate. Try to find different ways of interpreting or relating to the situation.

   b. Think dialectically. Shift black-and-white/all-or-nothing thoughts into a more balanced perspective.

   c. Act Opposite. Do the opposite of what the emotion is telling you to do, if the action would be harmful for you or your goals. Use skills (e.g., Distress Tolerance) as needed, too.

3. **Accept the problem.**

   a. Radically Accept. Practice accepting the situation with your full body and mind, even if you hate it, or you're not okay with it. Use Willing Hands and Half-Smiling.

   b. Distract and Self-Soothe. Use Crisis Survival skills. Engage in safe, nourishing, or distracting activities that help you tolerate the distress as long as it lasts.

   c. Practice Self-Compassion. Be gentle with yourself when suffering. Practice Nonjudgmentally, self-validation, and loving kindness. Practice Mindfulness of Current Emotions.

4. **Stay miserable.**

   You can choose to keep doing what you've been doing, do nothing, or not use any DBT skills—but only if you are willing to stay miserable!

5. **Make things worse.**

   You can choose to engage in impulsive or problematic behaviors that might help you feel some relief quickly—but only if you're okay with the original problem continuing and your behaviors potentially causing other problems (e.g., guilt/shame, disappointing others, physical health effects, increasing your emotional sensitivity in the long term, etc.).

Finally, keep trying. Often, you'll have to switch back and forth between options 1, 2, and 3. The options usually work best in some sort of combination, based on what is happening right now. Each new moment brings something new. Change is constant—keep experimenting!

Additional Resources

DBT Therapist Directories

Behavioral Tech
behavioraltech.org/resources/find-a-therapist

DBT-Linehan Board of Certification
dbt-lbc.org

Books

Building a Life Worth Living by Marsha Linehan

DBT Skills Training Handouts and Worksheets: Second Edition by Marsha Linehan

The High-Conflict Couple: A Dialectical Behavior Therapy Guide to Finding Peace, Intimacy, and Validation by Alan Fruzzetti

Loving Someone with Borderline Personality Disorder: How to Keep Out-of-Control Emotions from Destroying Your Relationship by Shari Manning

The Mindfulness Solution for Intense Emotions: Taking Control of Borderline Personality Disorder with DBT by Cedar Koons

Media about DBT Skills

Short Videos by The Dialectical Behavior Therapy Clinic at Rutgers University (DBT-RU)
youtube.com/c/DBTRU

To Hell and Back podcast by Charles Swenson
charlieswenson.com/podcasts

Therapists in the Wild podcast by Molly St. Denis and Liza Pincus
therapistsinthewild.com

The Skillful Podcast by Marielle Berg
bayareadbtcc.com/podcast

Emotion Vocabulary Resources

Atlas of the Heart by Brené Brown

The Atlas of Emotions
atlasofemotions.org

DBT Community Resources

"DBT Self Help" Online Peer Support
reddit.com/r/dbtselfhelp

The Family Connections Program
borderlinepersonalitydisorder.org/family-connections

Emotions Matter—Peer Resources Page
emotionsmatterbpd.org/peer-resources

Mindfulness Resources

Mindfulness and meditation apps: Headspace, Calm, Ten Percent Happier, BlackFULLness, Waking Up, and Insight Timer.

Tara Brach's website offers books, a podcast, and an online community.
tarabrach.com
cloudsangha.co

Sharon Salzberg's website offers books, a podcast, and other resources.
sharonsalzberg.com

The Insight Meditation Society offers meditation retreats and an online community.
dharma.org

UMass Memorial Health Center offers online mindfulness courses.
ummhealth.org/center-mindfulness

Scan this QR code to access downloadable copies of the worksheets found in this book.

References

Harned, M. S. (2022). *Treating Trauma in Dialectical Behavior Therapy: The DBT Prolonged Exposure Protocol (DBT PE).* New York: Guilford Press.

Linehan, M. M. (1993). *Cognitive-Behavioral Treatment of Borderline Personality Disorder.* New York: Guilford Press.

Linehan, M. M. (1993). *Skills Training Manual for Treating Borderline Personality Disorder.* New York: Guilford Press.

Linehan, M.M. (1997). Validation and psychotherapy. In A. Bohart & L. Greenberg (Eds.), *Empathy Reconsidered: New Directions in Psychotherapy.* Washington, DC: American Psychological Association, 353–392.

Linehan, M. M. (2015). *DBT Skills Training Handouts and Worksheets: Second Edition.* New York: Guilford Press.

Linehan, M. M. (2015). *DBT Skills Training Manual: Second Edition.* New York: Guilford Press.

Linehan, M. M. (2020). *Building a Life Worth Living.* New York: Random House.

Rizvi, S. L., Finkelstein, J., Wacha-Montes, A., Yeager, A. L., Ruork, A. K., Yin, Q., . . . & Kleiman, E. M. (2022). Randomized clinical trial of a brief, scalable intervention for mental health sequelae in college students during the COVID-19 pandemic. *Behaviour Research and Therapy,* 149, 104015.

Uliaszek, A. A., Rashid, T., Williams, G. E., & Gulamani, T. (2016). Group therapy for university students: A randomized control trial of dialectical behavior therapy and positive psychotherapy. *Behaviour Research and Therapy,* 77, 78–85.

About the Authors

 **Kiki Fehling, PhD,** is a licensed psychologist and DBT-Linehan Board of Certification, Certified Clinician™. Kiki specializes in borderline personality disorder, self-harming behaviors, and trauma, with particular expertise working with LGBTQ+ people. Kiki is passionate about helping people build meaningful lives through DBT. After witnessing the power of DBT skills in her own life and the lives of her clients, she is thrilled to share those skills through this book. You can follow them on TikTok, Instagram, and Twitter @dbtkiki.

 **Elliot Weiner, PhD,** is a licensed psychologist and the cofounder of New York Cognitive Behavioral Therapy (NYCBT) in New York City. He has expertise in dialectical behavior therapy as well as cognitive behavioral therapy and specializes in working with people with post-traumatic stress disorder and other difficulties related to trauma. Elliot is a DBT-Linehan Board of Certification, Certified Clinician™ and is Board Certified in Behavioral & Cognitive Psychology by the American Board of Professional Psychology. In his work as a clinical psychologist, Elliot is passionate about helping people learn practical strategies to decrease suffering and build more fulfilling, satisfying lives. Learn more at newyorkcbt.com.

Acknowledgments

Kiki Fehling

To my DBT teachers, Shireen Rizvi and Carrie Diamond, and my teams at DBT-RU, Montefiore, and NYCBT. You introduced me to a theoretical framework and philosophy that changed my life; thank you for supporting me tirelessly in this meaningful work. And, of course, my clients—your challenges have pushed me to become a better therapist, a better DBT skills teacher, and a better person; thank you for your vulnerability and courage.

To my coauthor, Elie. No one else balances acceptance and change, irreverence and warmth, quite like you. Thank you for making this writing process fun, and a very stressful time easier. I feel so fortunate to have had you as a coauthor, supervisor, colleague, and friend.

To our editors, Clara Song Lee, Sarah Curley, Amy Reed, and Kristen Bettcher. Writing a book has been one of my Life Worth Living goals—thank you for this opportunity! I'm immensely grateful for your guidance and feedback throughout this process.

Finally, to my family, Agusta, Claudia, Dan, Geoff, Henry, Marcia, and Rick—thank you, thank you, thank you.

Elliot Weiner

To my wife, Rachel. Thank you for encouraging and supporting me in this and everything, even when it was an especially inconvenient time for me to have extra work on my plate. And to Caleb and Sophie, for tolerating it when I was less available. You are the biggest parts of my Life Worth Living.

To Clara Song Lee, Sarah Curley, Amy Reed, and Kristen Bettcher, our editors. Thank you for giving us this opportunity, and for your thoughtful questions and suggestions throughout this process. As a first-time author, I have appreciated all your help and patience along the way.

To Kiki, thank you for embarking on this journey with me. Thank you also for your insightful comments and suggestions, which have helped me clarify and improve my contributions to this book immeasurably. You are a wonderful colleague, friend, and now coauthor, and I can't imagine writing this with anyone else.

Last but not least, thank you to all of the other therapists with whom I have participated on DBT teams over the years. I have learned DBT from you, most of all.

Index

Hi there,

We hope you enjoyed *Self-Directed DBT Skills*. If you have any questions or concerns about your book, or have received a damaged copy, please contact customerservice@penguinrandomhouse.com. We're here and happy to help.

Also, please consider writing a review on your favorite retailer's website to let others know what you thought of the book!

Sincerely,
The Zeitgeist Team